the
vegetable gardener's
cookbook

the
vegetable gardener's
cookbook

75 *Vegetarian Recipes That Will Help You Make the Most Out of Every Season's Harvest*

danielle majeika, *Founder of The Perpetual Season*

PAGE STREET
PUBLISHING CO.

PAGE STREET
PUBLISHING CO.

Copyright © 2019 Danielle Majeika

First published in 2019 by
Page Street Publishing Co.
27 Congress Street, Suite 105
Salem, MA 01970
www.pagestreetpublishing.com

Distributed by Macmillan, sales in Canada by The Canadian Manda Group.

23 22 21 20 19   1 2 3 4 5

ISBN-13: 978-1-62414-717-3
ISBN-10: 1-62414-717-8

Library of Congress Control Number: 2018953089

Cover and book design by Laura Gallant for Page Street Publishing Co.
Photography by Danielle Majeika

Printed and Bound in China

dedicated to those I have fervently loved, bravely do love and brazenly will love

autumn • 101

winter • 137

introduction

What moves you? A favorite question to ask and be asked; perhaps the only question there truly is.

As long as I can remember—my memory surely laced with all that's wistful and wild—the flux of seasons has been my greatest romance. A love unweathered by time and hinged on change, no doubt an auspicious cocktail. In recent years I have turned to gardening to celebrate this enchantment.

I will readily admit that the benefits of growing your own food are expansive. You are not only committing to your health, you are committing to the Earth and to humanity. From garden roots to the kitchen table is a path I've traveled well, and one I encourage you to traverse too. The true command of heart is working beside the seasons, growing what they govern and living in synergy.

Enclosed I've compiled gardening tips and a rather spirited collection of vegetarian recipes to offer you inspiration in the kitchen as you revel in your own bounty, whether from your own garden or the farmers' market.

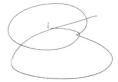

spring

The breeze barely murmurs, but the feeling is all-consuming. A hint of green buds fat on the trees, and the sun finds them with long, unfolded arms. The dusk is a taxi to renewed notions of regeneration and growth. Shoveling in a warm evening under the light of the rising moon uncovers deeply rooted earthworms, cycling through the soil with repetition and grace. We stir from our snowy blanket one morning and find we are surrounded by perseverance—a shift both gradual and dramatic.

There is an abundance of produce that is eager to embrace this very shift. Ambitious volunteers that will brave final frosts. Do not be afraid to plant peas, onions, spinach, radishes, lettuce and herbs come early spring. Start carrots and beets, and you will be rewarded with the ability to enjoy multiple crops throughout the season. Look for workable ground that's no longer frozen with a soil temperature between 40 to 45°F (4 to 7°C), and do not fear the imminent snow.

The food of spring is both celebratory and verdant, offering a nod to newness and growth. From this chapter, might I recommend seeking young, tender carrots and transforming them into a delightfully sweet and spicy hummus; paying homage to the sweet and delicate taste of peas by whirring them into a buttery soup; or piling fresh spring vegetables onto a bed of herbed ricotta flatbread.

asparagus with blood orange brown butter

In the fleeting moments that bridge the very end of winter with the beginning days of spring is a window of opportunity. Enjoy the last of the winter citrus, in this case, sweet-tart blood oranges, and marry them to the burgeoning firsts of the new season. The berry-like notes of the blood orange pair well with the richness of brown butter, creating a sauce that enhances the natural sweetness of roasted asparagus.

serves 4

1 bunch of asparagus (about 1 lb [454 g]), trimmed

2 tbsp (30 ml) extra-virgin olive oil

Kosher salt and fresh black pepper

4 tbsp (56 g) (½ stick) unsalted butter

1 medium shallot, minced

¼ cup (60 ml) fresh blood orange juice

Torn fresh mint, for serving

Preheat the oven to 450°F (232°C).

Set a roasting rack on the inside of a baking sheet and top it with the asparagus. Drizzle the olive oil over it, add a few generous pinches of salt and pepper and toss to coat. Place it in the oven and roast until crisp-tender, 8 to 10 minutes.

Meanwhile, melt the butter in a medium skillet over moderate heat. As soon as the butter begins to foam, add the minced shallot. Cook until the shallot becomes golden and the butter turns pale brown with a nutty fragrance, 3 to 5 minutes. As the butter begins to foam for a second time, add the blood orange juice and cook an additional minute, until slightly thickened.

Transfer the asparagus to a platter, drizzle it with the brown butter and top with torn mint.

tip: If the idea of a perennial vegetable excites you (and you're stationary), consider planting asparagus crowns early one spring season. Exercise patience, as asparagus takes a few seasons to mature, and any harvesting done before then may be detrimental to the final reward: successive spring harvests for as many as 30 years.

spicy roasted carrot hummus

I have an affinity for matching my vegetables with a trace of heat, and carrots are no stranger to this practice. Not only do they emulate hummus exceptionally well, I find that they elevate it. Serve this at room temperature with additional vegetables and pita.

serves 4–6

2 medium carrots

1 large clove garlic

1 tsp sesame oil

Pinch of salt, plus more to taste

1½ cups (246 g) cooked chickpeas (or 1 [15-oz (425-g)] can), drained and rinsed, plus more for serving

¼ cup (70 g) tahini

3 tbsp (45 ml) fresh lemon juice

1 tbsp (16 g) chili paste, such as sambal oelek

¼ tsp cumin

¼ tsp coriander

2 tbsp (30 ml) extra-virgin olive oil, plus more for serving

Chopped parsley and sesame seeds, for serving

Preheat the oven to 425°F (218°C).

Line a roasting pan with parchment paper and spread out the carrots and garlic clove. Toss them with the sesame oil and a small pinch of salt. Roast the carrots until tender, 40 to 50 minutes. Allow them to cool to room temperature.

Process the roasted carrots, garlic, chickpeas, tahini, lemon juice, chili paste, cumin and coriander in a food processor until the mixture is smooth, about 1 minute. With the motor running, stream in the olive oil until the hummus is light and creamy. Season to taste with salt.

Serve the hummus in a shallow bowl and garnish with parsley, sesame seeds, chickpeas and a drizzle of olive oil. Store the hummus in the refrigerator for 5 to 7 days.

radish tartine with pistachio-herb butter

The beauty of plucking radishes from the ground is their readiness to be enjoyed on the spot. My favorite way to eat a radish will forever be raw, so as not to mute their peppered crunch. A classic combination is with bread, butter and a hint of salt.

serves 4

½ cup (115 g) (1 stick) unsalted butter, softened

½ bunch of fresh chives

¼ cup (10 g) packed fresh flat-leaf parsley

¼ cup (10 g) packed fresh dill

2 tbsp (15 g) finely chopped pistachios

1 tsp fresh lemon juice

½ tsp finely grated lemon zest

½ tsp kosher salt, plus more for serving

¼ tsp fresh black pepper

4 slices thick-cut bread, toasted

1 bunch (10–12) of radishes, thinly shaved

Add the butter, chives, parsley, dill, pistachios, lemon juice, lemon zest, salt and pepper to a food processor and combine until smooth.

To serve, slather a slice of toasted bread generously with the herb butter. Top with the shaved radish slices, and finish with a final seasoning of salt.

tip: Sow radishes early and often, about every 10 days starting a few weeks before your final frost date. Do not leave them in the ground to get too big as their texture will degrade and they'll often crack. Use their greens to complement a garden salad or make them into a soup.

buttermilk-fried scallions with kimchi yogurt

With the first of a few fried recipes in this book, I must admit that I am not shy about battering my vegetables. They take exceptionally well to it. Fresh bunches of scallions are dressed in buttermilk, fried and dipped in kimchi-laced yogurt for a pleasantly funky kick.

serves 4–6

1 cup (245 g) plain Greek yogurt

1 cup (150 g) kimchi

1 tsp kosher salt, plus more for yogurt and serving

1 cup (125 g) all-purpose flour

½ cup (85 g) cornmeal

1 tsp garlic powder

½ tsp baking powder

¼ tsp cayenne

1½ cups (360 ml) buttermilk

½ bunch of fresh chives, minced

Canola oil, for frying

¾ lb (340 g) scallions (2–3 bunches)

To make the kimchi yogurt, combine the Greek yogurt, kimchi and a pinch of salt together and process in a food processor until smooth.

In a medium bowl, whisk together the flour, cornmeal, salt, garlic powder, baking powder and cayenne. Add the buttermilk and whisk until the mixture is blended and has the consistency of thick cream. Stir in the chives.

Pour the canola oil into a large saucepan to a depth of 2 inches (5 cm) and heat over medium-high heat to 350°F (175°C). Line a baking sheet with a layer of paper towels.

Trim off the root ends and cut away the dark green ends of the scallions. Using tongs, dip the scallions into the batter. Working in batches, fry the scallions until golden brown, 4 to 5 minutes. Transfer the scallions to the paper towels and season immediately with salt.

Serve hot with the kimchi yogurt.

arugula & radish salad with scallion vinaigrette

I find salad dressing to be a rewarding venture when made at home—the possibilities are truly endless, and the results are unbeatably fresh. Here, blended spring scallions offer an aromatic addition to a toss of peppery spring arugula and spicy slices of radish. Feel free to use this dressing as a complement to steamed vegetables or cooked grains as well.

makes about ¾ cup (180 ml)

4 scallions, pale green and white parts, coarsely chopped

2 tbsp (30 ml) white wine vinegar

1 tbsp (16 g) Dijon mustard

¾ cup (180 ml) extra-virgin olive oil

Kosher salt and fresh black pepper, to taste

5 bunches of arugula (about 1¼ lb [567 g])

1 bunch of radishes (about 8 oz [227 g]), sliced

In a blender, purée the scallions, vinegar and mustard. Slowly stream in the olive oil until the mixture is emulsified; season to taste with salt and pepper. Add two-thirds of the dressing to the bottom of a large serving bowl. Add the arugula and the radishes to the bowl and toss well to coat. Taste the salad and add more dressing if needed. Serve the salad immediately.

tip: Scallions are a bunching perennial that will enthusiastically multiply and come back from any you didn't harvest the season before, which makes them a prime candidate for any home garden. The beauty of scallions is that you can grow them and take only what is needed.

charred snap peas with chive vinaigrette & whipped ricotta

A brief affair with high heat is a dependable method for searing the sweetness of the pea into itself. The crisp-tender, slightly smoky peas are brightened by a lemony chive vinaigrette, making them the perfect partner for luscious and spicy whipped ricotta.

serves 4

¼ cup (60 ml) plus 1 tsp extra-virgin olive oil, divided

1 lb (454 g) sugar snap peas

2 tsp (10 g) Dijon mustard

2 tsp (10 ml) fresh lemon juice

2 tbsp (6 g) minced fresh chives

Pinch of kosher salt and fresh black pepper

¾ cup (186 g) whole-milk ricotta

½ tsp finely grated lemon zest

Pinch of crushed red pepper

¼ cup (10 g) mint leaves, finely chopped

Heat 2 tablespoons (30 ml) of the olive oil in a large skillet over medium-high heat. Add the snap peas and cook, stirring occasionally, until crisp-tender and lightly charred, 3 to 5 minutes

Combine the mustard, lemon juice and chives in a small bowl along with a pinch of salt and pepper. Whisk in 2 tablespoons (30 ml) of the olive oil until well blended.

In a large bowl, toss the snap peas with the vinaigrette.

In a food processor, combine the ricotta, remaining teaspoon of olive oil, lemon zest and crushed red pepper. Whip the ricotta until smooth. Remove the mixture from the food processor and fold in the mint leaves.

To serve, smear the ricotta on a platter and top it with the charred snap peas. Serve the snap peas with thick slices of toasted bread or alongside a slice of flatbread or pizza.

tip: Legumes are a great source of nitrogen. Enjoy an early, cool season crop of peas—they are one of spring's most tenacious forces. While they can be cultivated in the summer, their pods yield a crisp sweetness when allowed to mature in cool temperatures.

fresh herb salad with poached marcona almonds

Passels of fresh spring herbs make for an enticing and abundant salad infused with sweet, anisey, peppery notes that are supported by buttery, rich oil-poached almonds. Include the most tender and green leaves to assemble a salad that would perform equally well as an appetizer, accompaniment or palate cleanser.

serves 4

1 small shallot, minced

2 tbsp (30 ml) fresh lemon juice

1 tbsp (15 ml) white wine vinegar

2 tsp (10 g) Dijon mustard

Kosher salt and fresh black pepper, to taste

1 cup (240 ml) extra-virgin olive oil, divided

4 oz (113 g) Marcona almonds

1 bunch of fresh chives, chopped

1 cup (40 g) torn fresh flat-leaf parsley

1 cup (40 g) torn fresh dill

1 cup (40 g) torn fresh basil

½ cup (20 g) torn fresh mint

1 small fennel bulb, cored and thinly sliced lengthwise

1 cup (20 g) arugula

In a jar with a lid, combine the shallot, lemon juice, vinegar and mustard. Season with salt and pepper. Close the lid and shake the jar well to mix. Add ½ cup (120 ml) of the olive oil and continue to shake well until the mixture is emulsified.

In a small skillet, heat the remaining ½ cup (120 ml) of olive oil and add the almonds. Cook over low heat until golden, 15 to 20 minutes. Remove the almonds to a paper towel–lined plate and season immediately with salt.

To prepare the salad, combine the herbs, fennel bulb, arugula and almonds, and drizzle them lightly with the dressing.

tip: To proliferate your bounty, try looking into companion planting as a different avenue to laying out your vegetable garden. Planting tall vegetables with shade-loving vegetables can extend your harvest and help you use your space to its fullest capacity. Other groupings may mutually benefit one another in the way of nutrients, flavor and pest repellent. Whether you have a plot, or perhaps grow in pots, companion planting lets you produce freely and intensively—allowing for a truly endless season, ripe with fruition and delight.

mustard-butter roasted radishes with herbs

While I've already admitted my unrelenting affection for raw radishes, roasting them comes in as a curious second appeal. This preparation mellows their bite, and leaves you with a crispy, but juicy pop that is hard to dismiss. Lemon juice and a collection of fresh herbs work to brighten the warmth introduced to the radishes. Serve these radishes as a side dish, or pile them on top of the Spring Flatbreads with Herbed Ricotta (page 42) for a welcomed rendition.

serves 4

1 lb (454 g) radishes, halved or quartered if very large

1 tbsp (15 ml) extra-virgin olive oil

Kosher salt, to taste

¼ cup (56 g) (½ stick) unsalted butter

1 tsp Dijon mustard

1 tsp lemon juice

Minced fresh herbs, such as tarragon, parsley, mint, dill, chives

Preheat the oven to 425°F (218°C). Line a rimmed baking sheet with aluminum foil.

In a medium bowl, drizzle the radishes lightly with the olive oil, tossing to coat, and season well with salt. Arrange the radishes in an even layer on the baking sheet, and roast them in the oven, stirring once halfway through, until the radishes are crisp-tender and browned, 20 to 25 minutes.

Melt the butter in a medium skillet over low heat. Stir in the mustard and lemon juice. Add the radishes and toss to coat. Remove them from the heat and stir in a medley of mixed minced herbs.

tip: The weather has a lot to do with the spiciness of a radish—a hot and dry season will encourage it.

kale & avocado salad with carrot-miso-ginger dressing

Miso is an enjoyable accompaniment to the inherent sweetness of carrots—it generates a buttery, sweetness-enhancing umami. The sharpness of the ginger is balanced by the nutty sesame oil and mellowed with the carrot-miso union. Although a slightly thicker dressing, this is a perfect complement to a bed of robust kale and creamy avocado.

serves 4

¼ cup (60 ml) grapeseed oil (or other neutral oil)

¼ cup (60 ml) rice wine vinegar

1 medium carrot, coarsely chopped

1 tbsp (17 g) white miso

1 (1" [3-cm]) piece ginger, peeled and coarsely chopped

2 tsp (10 ml) sesame oil

Kosher salt and fresh black pepper, to taste

1 tbsp (10 g) toasted sesame seeds

1 large bunch of kale, stemmed and coarsely chopped

1 avocado, halved and sliced

⅓ cup (40 g) toasted almonds, coarsely chopped

Make the dressing by adding the oil, vinegar, carrot, miso, ginger and sesame oil to a food processor and processing until very smooth; season to taste with salt and pepper. Stir in the sesame seeds.

In a large bowl, toss the kale, avocado and almonds together. Add a quarter of the prepared carrot dressing, and toss to coat. Add more if desired and serve.

tip: Carrot seed varieties are often divided into categories based on their shape. The easiest and most common variety for home gardeners are Nantes type carrots—they are quick to grow and mature. Also look out for Imperator, Chantenay and Mini varieties.

salt-roasted fingerlings with green goddess dressing

Salt roasting potatoes encases them with a warmth that yields addictively crispy skins and irresistibly creamy innards. Once they're roasted, brush the excess salt from the skins and dip the potatoes in an herby, zippy, green goddess dressing to complete the very portrait of spring.

serves 4

1½ cups (200 g) kosher salt, plus more to taste

2 tbsp (30 ml) extra-virgin olive oil

1½ lbs (680 g) fingerling potatoes

¼ cup (60 ml) buttermilk

1 cup (40 g) fresh flat-leaf parsley

1 cup (40 g) stemmed watercress

½ cup (20 g) fresh basil leaves

3 tbsp (9 g) minced fresh chives

2 tbsp (6 g) chopped fresh tarragon

1 clove garlic

1 tbsp (15 ml) fresh lemon juice

½ cup (110 g) mayonnaise

Fresh black pepper, to taste

Preheat the oven to 425°F (218°C).

Stir together the salt and oil in a shallow baking dish. Add the potatoes and rub them with the oil mixture to coat them. Roast them until the flesh is tender and the skins are crisp, 45 to 50 minutes.

Meanwhile, combine the buttermilk, parsley, watercress, basil, chives, tarragon, garlic and lemon juice in a blender or food processor. Blend until smooth, 2 minutes. Add the mayonnaise and blend again until smooth. Season to taste with salt and pepper.

Serve the potatoes hot with a side of green goddess dressing.

shaved asparagus salad

Asparagus is just as delightful when freshly shaved and enjoyed in a salad of equally sweet and savory proportions. Long, shaved spears mingle with the peppery bite of arugula, awaken with the vigor of lemon, flirt with the sweetness of peas—take a bite with raw red onion and soothe with creamy, salty feta. This salad is a reminder that fresh ingredients need very little to create a great and memorable sum of parts.

serves 4

2 tbsp (15 g) pine nuts

1 lb (454 g) thick green asparagus

¼ cup (60 ml) extra-virgin olive oil

3 tbsp (45 ml) fresh lemon juice

Kosher salt and fresh black pepper, to taste

8 oz (227 g) arugula

½ cup (75 g) shelled fresh green peas, thawed if frozen

¼ small red onion, sliced thin

4 oz (113 g) feta cheese, crumbled

1 tbsp (3 g) chopped fresh mint

In a small skillet over medium heat, toast the pine nuts, stirring often, until lightly browned, about 5 minutes. Remove from the heat and cool.

Snap off and discard the tough ends of the asparagus. Shave the asparagus into paper-thin ribbons.

In a small bowl, whisk together the olive oil and lemon juice to make a dressing. Season to taste with salt and pepper.

Transfer the asparagus ribbons to a large, shallow serving bowl and coat them with half of the dressing. Add the arugula, peas, red onion, feta, mint and pine nuts and toss to combine. Season to taste with additional salt and pepper. Drizzle the salad with the remaining dressing and serve immediately.

fresh pea soup with arugula salsa verde

If ever there was a remedy for winter-worn spirits, may I profess it to be peas. They are eager and tenacious volunteers in early spring's frost-laden throes. Enter a celebratory soup. By simmering fresh peas for a very short amount of time, it's easy to preserve their vibrant hue and sweet essence. Add a lemony, nutty, peppery bite of arugula salsa into each bowl of soup to introduce a surprising but welcomed zip to each spoonful.

serves 4–6

2 tbsp (28 g) unsalted butter

3 medium shallots, sliced thin

Pinch of kosher salt, plus more to taste

2 cloves garlic, minced, plus 1 whole clove garlic

1 cup (20 g) arugula leaves

1 cup (40 g) fresh flat-leaf parsley

1 tsp finely grated lemon zest

2 tbsp (30 ml) fresh lemon juice

½ cup (120 ml) extra-virgin olive oil

Fresh black pepper, to taste

4 cups (580 g) shelled fresh peas, thawed if frozen

Melt the butter in a large soup pot over medium-high heat. Add the shallots with a pinch of salt, and cook over medium heat until the shallots are soft and translucent. Add the minced garlic and cook an additional minute, until fragrant. Add 4 cups (960 ml) of water and bring to a boil. Reduce the heat and simmer, covered, for 30 minutes.

Meanwhile, make the salsa verde. In a food processor, pulse the whole garlic clove, arugula, parsley, lemon zest, lemon juice and olive oil until relatively smooth; season with salt and pepper.

To the large soup pot, add the peas with salt and pepper to taste, and bring the soup back to a boil. Simmer the peas for 5 minutes and then remove the soup from the heat to cool. Purée the soup, in batches if necessary, until smooth. Strain the soup through a fine-mesh sieve and return it to the stove to warm. Season with additional salt if needed.

Serve hot with a generous swirl of salsa verde.

tip: While many sources advise you to plant a thin sowing of peas, I've always sowed them thick and with great reward. Peas enjoy climbing, but if you do not have a trellis to support them, simply use the brush from pruned trees or bushes. Once the peas have finished their cycle, till the vines back into the soil to enjoy the nitrogen-fixing benefits.

cream of almond leek soup with frizzled leeks

Sautéed leeks and almonds are blended together to create a comforting, rich and super creamy soup without the use of any dairy. Top the soup with copious amounts of frizzled leeks for a crispy, contrasting pop and an extra dose of this beloved allium.

serves 4–6

cream of almond leek soup

¼ cup (60 ml) extra-virgin olive oil

4 large leeks, white and pale green parts, sliced

Pinch of kosher salt, plus more to taste

4 cloves garlic, minced

6 cups (1.4 L) vegetable stock, plus more for thinning

1½ cups (215 g) raw almonds

1 tsp crushed red pepper

1 bay leaf

1 tbsp (15 ml) fresh lemon juice

Fresh black pepper, to taste

frizzled leeks

2 medium leeks, trimmed

3 cups (720 ml) canola oil

Kosher salt

In a large soup pot, heat the olive oil over medium heat and add the sliced leeks along with a generous pinch of salt. Cook, stirring, until the leeks are wilted and tender, 5 to 8 minutes. Add the garlic and cook an additional minute, until fragrant. Add the vegetable stock, almonds, crushed red pepper and bay leaf. Bring to a boil, reduce the heat and simmer, covered, for 30 minutes. Taste and adjust the salt as necessary. Discard the bay leaf. Remove the soup from the heat and let cool.

Strain the soup through a fine-mesh sieve. If you find the soup very thick, thin it with a little water to achieve a pourable consistency. Return the soup to the stove.

Stir the lemon juice into the soup; season with additional salt and pepper and warm the soup over medium-low heat.

To make the frizzled leeks, thinly slice the white and pale-green parts of the leeks lengthwise into 3-inch (8-cm) strips. In a small saucepan, heat the oil over medium-high heat until it reaches 350°F (175°C)—maintain this temperature while frying. Working in batches, fry the leeks until golden, 30 to 60 seconds, and transfer them to a paper towel–lined plate to dry. Season the hot leeks with salt.

Serve the soup topped with frizzled leeks.

tip: Enjoy sowing and harvesting leeks year-round. They are tolerant of all weather and there are varieties available for every season.

asparagus, spinach & goat cheese frittata

Nothing signifies spring like a generous, fresh frittata, brimming with the garden's abundance. The beauty of it is the endless template it provides, though here I offer it to you with fresh asparagus, spinach, an assemblage of herbs and sublimely rich goat cheese. This frittata is perfectly suited for breakfast or brunch, yet hearty enough to enjoy for dinner.

serves 4–6

8 large eggs

Pinch of kosher salt and freshly ground black pepper

2 tbsp (30 ml) cream

½ cup (20 g) packed fresh basil leaves, thinly sliced

3 tbsp (9 g) minced fresh chives

1 lb (454 g) asparagus, thinly sliced

2 tbsp (30 ml) extra-virgin olive oil

2 medium shallots, finely chopped

1 clove garlic, minced

3 cups (90 g) spinach

4 oz (113 g) goat cheese, crumbled

Preheat the oven to 425°F (218°C).

In a medium bowl, whisk the eggs together with a pinch of salt and pepper and the cream. Stir in the basil leaves, chives and sliced asparagus.

Heat the olive oil in a 10-inch (25-cm) ovenproof skillet over medium-high heat. Add the shallots and garlic, and cook, stirring occasionally, until they are softened, 3 to 5 minutes. Add the spinach, a handful at a time, and stir until it's wilted.

Pour the egg mixture into the skillet. Reduce the heat and cook until the edges have set and are beginning to color, 5 minutes. The center will still be loose. Dollop the goat cheese over the top of the eggs.

Transfer the skillet to the oven, and bake until the top is puffed and the eggs are completely set, 10 to 15 minutes.

Allow the frittata to rest for 10 minutes before serving.

tip: Spinach thrives in the spring and fall, when cooler temperatures won't cause it to bolt. It is a hardy presence in the garden, and seeds will germinate through intermittent early snowfalls. Enjoy it early, young and fresh. If a heat wave is coming your way, pull the spinach leaves and enjoy them before they have a chance to become bitter.

orecchiette with peas, pea greens & parmesan

Orecchiette offers itself as the perfect shape for fresh peas, perfectly encapsulating the sweet, green pearls. Make clever and celebratory use of tender, young pea shoots by tossing them with a cheesy, starchy pan sauce kissed with a spicy, grassy, sweet trio of herbs.

serves 4–6

1 lb (454 g) orecchiette

1 lb (454 g) shelled fresh peas, thawed if frozen (about ¾ cup [100 g])

6 oz (170 g) pea greens (tendrils, shoots)

1 tbsp (15 ml) extra-virgin olive oil

1 large clove garlic, minced

1 bunch of scallions, light green and white parts, finely chopped

½ cup (50 g) freshly grated Parmesan

Fresh black pepper, to taste

1 tbsp (3 g) minced fresh chives

1 tbsp (3 g) chopped fresh parsley

1 tbsp (3 g) chopped fresh mint

Cook the orecchiette in a large pot of boiling salted water until al dente, using the package instructions as a reference. Drain the pasta, reserving 1 cup (240 ml) of the pasta cooking water.

Refill the pot with 1 inch (3 cm) of water and bring it to a boil. Steam the peas in a steamer basket until just tender, about 4 minutes, and transfer them to a bowl. Add the pea tendrils to the steamer basket and steam them an additional 2 minutes until wilted. Cool slightly, squeeze the excess water from the pea tendrils and coarsely chop them.

Heat the olive oil in a large skillet over medium-high heat and add the garlic and scallions. Cook, stirring, until the scallions wilt, about 3 minutes. Add the peas and pea tendrils and toss to combine. Add the pasta along with the reserved pasta water and the Parmesan. Season with pepper to taste. Cook over medium-high heat until the sauce has thickened and is creamy, about 2 minutes. Stir in the fresh chives, parsley and mint. Serve immediately.

spring flatbreads with herbed ricotta

Layer oven-baked chickpea flatbreads with the freshest produce that spring has to offer. A combination of asparagus and snap peas is sautéed until crisp-tender and sweet and is introduced to a lemony, fluffy bed of herbaceous ricotta punctuated by salty, briny capers.

makes 2 flatbreads, serves 4–6

2 cups (185 g) garbanzo bean flour, plus more for dusting

1 tsp baking powder

1 tsp kosher salt, plus more for seasoning

6 tbsp (90 ml) extra-virgin olive oil, divided

1 cup (248 g) fresh ricotta

2 tbsp (30 ml) fresh lemon juice

½ tsp finely grated lemon zest

1 clove garlic, finely grated

½ cup (20 g) finely chopped mixed fresh herbs (chives, dill, parsley, mint), plus more for serving

Fresh black pepper, to taste

½ bunch of thick asparagus, chopped

2 cups (200 g) sugar snap peas

2 tbsp (18 g) capers

Preheat the oven to 400°F (200°C) with a baking stone or inverted baking sheet placed inside.

In a large bowl, whisk together the flour, baking powder and 1 teaspoon of salt. Drizzle in 2 tablespoons (30 ml) of olive oil and, using your hands, combine until the mixture becomes crumbly. Add up to ½ cup (120 ml) of water, 1 tablespoon (15 ml) at a time, until you have a uniform and pliable dough. Knead the dough until smooth, 3 to 5 minutes. Form it into a ball, cover it with a damp kitchen towel and let it rest for 10 minutes.

Divide the dough into two equal pieces. Roll them out on a sheet of parchment paper and lightly dust them with flour. Working with 1 piece of dough at a time (reserve the other beneath the damp towel), roll it out on top of the parchment paper into a disc shape ¼ inch (6 mm) thick. Dust the top of the flatbread with additional flour to prevent sticking.

Carefully remove the heated baking sheet from the oven and transfer the dough onto it. Bake for 10 to 12 minutes, until light brown and crisp. Repeat with the remaining dough.

While the flatbreads are baking, purée the ricotta with the lemon juice, lemon zest, garlic and 2 tablespoons (30 ml) of olive oil in a food processor until smooth. Stir in the herbs, and season with salt and pepper.

Heat 1 tablespoon (15 ml) of olive oil in a medium skillet over medium-high heat. Add the asparagus and snap peas, and sauté until crisp-tender, 3 to 5 minutes.

Assemble the flatbreads with the ricotta, asparagus, snap peas, capers and additional herbs. Drizzle with the remaining tablespoon (15 ml) of olive oil, and sprinkle with salt and pepper.

baked falafel with pickled onions & lemon tahini sauce

Ground split peas are combined with fresh peas, herbs, pistachios and spices to form a verdant take on falafel dough. Instead of frying, pop them in the oven to bake for a light, but satisfying meal. Any fresh greens you have on hand would be perfect with a few falafels laced with vinegary red onions and rich, creamy tahini sauce.

serves 4–6

½ cup (120 ml) apple cider vinegar

1 tbsp (12 g) granulated sugar

2½ tsp (7 g) kosher salt, divided, plus more for seasoning

1 red onion, thinly sliced

½ cup (98 g) dried green split peas

6 sprigs of fresh cilantro

6 sprigs of fresh mint

6 sprigs of fresh parsley

½ cup (60 g) shelled pistachios

1½ cups (228 g) shelled fresh peas, thawed if frozen

½ cup (80 g) coarsely chopped onion

1 tbsp (8 g) garbanzo bean flour (or another flour of choice)

2 cloves garlic, minced, plus 1 clove garlic, grated

1 tsp ground coriander

1 tsp ground cumin

½ tsp baking powder

½ cup (140 g) sesame tahini

2 tbsp (30 ml) extra-virgin olive oil

2 tbsp (30 ml) fresh lemon juice

¼ tsp cayenne powder

Kale, collard, Swiss chard leaves or pita, for serving

Chopped tomatoes and thinly sliced cucumber, for serving

Begin by making the pickled red onions: whisk together the apple cider vinegar, sugar, 1½ teaspoons (4 g) of salt and 1 cup (240 ml) of water in a medium bowl until the salt and sugar have dissolved. Place the sliced red onion in a medium-size jar and pour the vinegar mixture over it. Allow it to stand at room temperature for at least 1 hour before serving.

Grind the dried split peas into a fine powder; reserve. Lightly pulse the cilantro, mint and parsley in a food processor. Add the pistachios, and pulse a few times to finely chop. Add the fresh peas, and pulse a few more times to chop. Add the ground split peas, chopped onion, garbanzo bean flour, minced garlic, coriander, cumin, baking powder and 1 teaspoon of salt, and process until combined but still a tad rough, scraping down the sides as necessary.

Using your hands, form 15 small, round falafels. Place them on a parchment-lined baking sheet and refrigerate them until firm.

Preheat the oven to 375°F (190°C). Bake the falafels for about 15 to 20 minutes, until the tops are crisp.

Meanwhile, make the lemon tahini sauce. Whisk together the tahini, olive oil, lemon juice, 2 tablespoons (30 ml) of water, the remaining grated garlic clove and the cayenne pepper; season to taste with salt. Thin with additional water if necessary.

Serve the baked falafel in leaf wraps or pita with pickled red onions, tomato, cucumber and a drizzle of tahini sauce.

golden beet lemonade

Beets, innately sweet in nature, lend themselves well to juicing and, here, to lemonade. The earthiness of the beet poses as a natural companion for the acidic tang of lemon. Add the honey as you see fit. You may come to find you do not need it at all.

makes 4 cups (960 ml)

½ lb (227 g) golden beets, peeled and quartered

2 medium lemons, piths removed and roughly chopped

2" (5-cm) piece fresh ginger, peeled and roughly chopped

4 cups (960 ml) chilled filtered water

Honey, to sweeten, to taste

Ice, for serving

Lemon peel, for garnish

Combine the beets, lemons, ginger and water in a blender, and blend on high for 1 minute, or until the mixture is smooth. Run the mixture through a fine-mesh sieve, pressing against the pulp with a spatula to extract as much liquid as possible.

Transfer to a pitcher to serve, adding honey for additional sweetness to taste. Serve over ice and garnished with a lemon peel.

celery-apple-cilantro juice

Affectionately, I would like to divulge to you that this is my favorite juice, one that I urge you to include in your repertoire as well. It satisfies on all fronts with freshness, zing, tartness, sweetness and herbs.

makes 2 cups (480 ml)

1 large green apple

1" (3-cm) piece fresh ginger, peeled

3 ribs celery

2 cups (32 g) packed fresh cilantro

2 tbsp (30 ml) apple cider vinegar

1 tsp honey

1½ cups (360 ml) filtered water

Ice

Add the apple, ginger, celery, cilantro, vinegar and honey to a blender along with the filtered water, and process until smooth. Strain the juice through a fine-mesh sieve, pressing into the solids with a spatula. Serve the strained juice over ice.

pea-mint sorbet

Nothing can play off of peas' saccharine sweetness quite like a fresh sorbet. Blanching the peas keeps this enjoyable asset intact and up-front. A sweet mint simple syrup infuses the sorbet with a decidedly spring palate. Enjoy this as a dessert or palate cleanser.

makes 1 quart (1 L)

4 cups (580 g) shelled fresh peas, thawed if frozen

1 cup (40 g) packed fresh mint leaves

1 cup (192 g) granulated sugar

1 tbsp (15 ml) fresh lemon juice

Bring a large pot of water to a boil over high heat, add the peas and boil them until they're bright green, 2 minutes. Drain the peas and immediately submerge them into a bath of ice water. Let the peas chill in the water for 2 minutes, and then drain them well once more.

Roughly chop the mint leaves, and combine them with the sugar and 1 cup (240 ml) of water in a medium saucepan. Bring the mixture to a boil, stirring occasionally, until the sugar has dissolved. Reduce the heat and simmer the syrup for 2 minutes. Remove it from the heat and steep it an additional 5 minutes. Pour the syrup through a fine-mesh sieve, pressing into the mint, and allow it to cool.

Process the peas and ¾ cup (180 ml) of the simple syrup (the remaining syrup will keep in the refrigerator for a few weeks) in a blender or food processor until smooth. Stir in the lemon juice. Cover and refrigerate the mixture until very cold, at least 1 hour or up to overnight. Pour the chilled mixture into an ice cream machine and prepare it according to the manufacturer's instructions. For a thicker consistency, freeze the sorbet for an additional 4 hours.

summer

In the slowness born of anticipation, summer often takes her time to arrive. Once here, she buries us deeply beneath a sultry gaze of lengthy days and endless nights. The summer exhibits tenacity in the garden—high and lush tides of tomatoes, peppers, cucumbers, eggplants and squash lapping at the back door. Summer's produce beckons for simplicity in cooking: a chance to depict wealth in ripeness and flavor.

You can procure this wealth in your own garden with some tricks I've learned along the way: simple extensions to your methods that will surely elevate the very heart of your harvest. Oftentimes, a sweeter, hotter or crisper yield is simply knowing the perfect moment and indulging in it.

Summer's recipes are a study in fruitful abundance; my favorites in this chapter include the indulgence of sweet corn fritters (page 56), the necessary simplicity of an open-faced tomato sandwich layered with marinated feta (page 84) and an irresistible summer dinner idea: a mega-savory roasted cherry tomato cobbler with Gruyère-blanketed and chive-studded biscuits (page 88).

sesame heirloom tomato salad with za'atar–corn bread croutons

Corn and tomatoes have a natural affinity for each other. Try to compose this salad with the freshest available, as you always should with simple assemblages. The deal is sweetened exponentially with hints of sesame and basil. The croutons work best with day-old corn bread, but can also be made with fresh bread if it's what you have on hand.

serves 4

2 cups (90 g) day-old corn bread, cubed in 1" (3-cm) pieces

2 tbsp (30 ml) extra-virgin olive oil

2 tsp (2 g) za'atar

¼ cup (60 ml) toasted sesame oil

2 tbsp (30 ml) rice vinegar

¼ tsp kosher salt

⅛ tsp fresh black pepper

2 lbs (907 g) heirloom tomatoes, chopped into 1" (3-cm) pieces

½ cup (20 g) fresh basil, sliced into ribbons

Preheat the oven to 400°F (200°C).

Toss the corn bread with the olive oil, and splay it out on a parchment-lined baking sheet. Sprinkle the za'atar over the corn bread, and toss to coat. Bake for 10 minutes, until crisp and browned.

In a small bowl, combine the sesame oil, rice vinegar, salt and pepper, and whisk vigorously to combine.

Toss the tomatoes and basil with the vinaigrette. Add the corn bread croutons, and toss to coat. Allow the salad to marinate for 20 minutes before serving.

tip: As tomatoes begin to ripen on the vine, a boost of potassium will deepen their sugars and sweeten their taste. Wood ash is an easy and accessible source you can apply directly to the base of your plants. Simply add it to the base and then water.

corn fritters with poblano pesto

Sweet and juicy corn kernels are stripped from the cob, dipped in a batter of cornmeal and flour, and then dipped in a hot oil bath. These fritters are an homage to the sizzling days of summer, never-ending and ripe with elation. Enjoy them dipped in a softly spicy pesto made from broiled poblanos. Alternatively, enjoy them dusted with confectioners' sugar or drizzled in maple syrup for a dessert-like take.

makes 2 dozen

2 large poblano peppers

½ medium yellow onion, halved

½ cup (120 ml) extra-virgin olive oil, divided

2 cloves garlic, smashed

¼ cup (4 g) fresh cilantro leaves

1 tbsp (15 ml) fresh lime juice

4 oz (113 g) cotija cheese

Kosher salt, to taste

½ cup (67 g) all-purpose flour

½ cup (85 g) yellow cornmeal

1 tsp granulated sugar

2 tsp (8 g) baking powder

Pinch of cayenne pepper

¾ cup (180 ml) whole milk

1 large egg, beaten

Kernels from 2 large ears of corn (about 2 cups [332 g] corn)

½ cup (20 g) fresh basil, finely chopped

Vegetable oil, for frying

Preheat the oven's broiler and position the rack in the upper third.

Line a baking sheet with aluminum foil, and toss the poblanos and onion with 1 tablespoon (15 ml) of olive oil. Broil, turning occasionally with tongs, until blackened on all sides, 6 to 8 minutes. Add the garlic, and broil an additional 2 minutes. Remove from the heat and allow to cool.

Peel, stem and seed the peppers and roughly chop. Transfer them to a food processor with the onion, garlic and cilantro. Pulse a few times until chopped. Add the remaining olive oil, lime juice and cotija cheese, and process until smooth. Season with salt.

For the fritters, in a large bowl, combine the flour, cornmeal, sugar, baking powder and cayenne pepper. Add the milk and egg, and stir to create a batter. If the batter is too thick, drizzle in extra milk until you have the consistency of a thick pancake batter. Fold in the corn and basil.

Pour the vegetable oil into a large saucepan to a depth of 3 inches (8 cm), and heat over medium-high heat to 350°F (175°C). Line a baking sheet with a layer of paper towels.

Working in batches, spoon tablespoons (15 ml) of the batter into the hot oil, making sure not to overcrowd. Fry, turning occasionally, until the fritters are golden brown on all sides, 2 to 4 minutes. Transfer the fritters to the paper towels and season immediately with salt.

Serve hot with the poblano pesto.

shaved zucchini salad with basil & olives

Zucchini's oblong shape lends itself well to fresh, raw ribbons. Shower the ribbons with fresh summer herbs, shaves of nutty Parmesan and bursts of pine nuts. There would be no harm in allowing this salad to marinate slightly beforehand to soak in the lemon juice, olive oil and brine from the olives. Serve this as a refreshing complement to a warm summer's evening, as well as a welcome departure from cooking in the heat.

serves 4–6

1½ lbs (680 g) zucchini, trimmed

½ cup (20 g) fresh basil, chopped

¼ cup (10 g) torn fresh mint leaves

1 cup (80 g) shaved aged Parmesan cheese

¼ cup (30 g) pine nuts, toasted

¼ cup (45 g) kalamata olives, chopped

3 tbsp (45 ml) extra-virgin olive oil

1 tbsp (15 ml) fresh lemon juice

½ tsp finely grated lemon zest

¼ tsp crushed red pepper

Kosher salt, to taste

Using a vegetable peeler or mandolin, shave the zucchini lengthwise into ribbons. In a large bowl, toss together the zucchini, basil, mint, Parmesan, pine nuts and olives.

Whisk together the olive oil, lemon juice, lemon zest and crushed red pepper until smooth. Season with salt. Toss the vinaigrette with the salad.

smoky baba ghanoush

Grilled eggplant imparts a smoky flavor essential to this savory Middle Eastern dip, but if you do not have access to a grill, you can get away with using your broiler. Serve this rich and creamy dip at room temperature with raw vegetables and pita.

serves 4–6

3 medium eggplants (about 2 lbs [907 g] total)

¼ cup (70 g) tahini

1 tsp kosher salt

3 tbsp (45 ml) fresh lemon juice

3 medium cloves garlic, roughly chopped

2 tbsp (30 g) plain Greek yogurt

Extra-virgin olive oil, for serving

Fresh parsley, for serving

Fresh mint, for serving

Preheat the grill for medium-high heat.

Prick the eggplants a few times with a fork or knife and place them directly over the heat. Grill, turning occasionally, until charred and soft, 25 to 35 minutes.

Split the eggplants in half lengthwise and scrape the pulp into a colander set over a bowl, discarding the skins. Allow the excess water from the pulp to drain, anywhere from 30 minutes to 1 hour. Discard the drained liquid.

Add the eggplant to a food processor along with the tahini, salt, lemon juice, garlic and Greek yogurt. Pulse until very smooth, and adjust the seasoning with additional salt if necessary.

Serve drizzled with good olive oil and showered with parsley and mint.

tip: Eggplant, a shrub of tropical heritage, bears an array of colorful and oddly shaped fruit, perfect for stir-fries, stews and as a shining star all on its own. The lighter the skin color of the variety, the milder the taste. Look to the skin for indications of when to harvest—if the seeds within have browned, your harvest is too late and will result in bitterness. Pull the eggplant once the skin is glossy and smooth and, for larger varieties, once it springs back to the touch.

grated tomato vinaigrette on a bed of greens

Grating tomatoes is an intriguing and clever technique if you do not own a mill. Here, it provides a delicious vinaigrette with hints of sherry, lemon juice, mustard and parsley. Try serving this salad with crusty bread for a light summer meal.

makes about 1 cup (240 ml)

1 medium heirloom tomato (about ¾ lb [340 g])

½ cup (120 ml) extra-virgin olive oil

1 tbsp (15 ml) sherry vinegar

1 tbsp (15 ml) fresh lemon juice

½ tbsp (8 g) Dijon mustard

1 tbsp (3 g) chopped fresh parsley

Kosher salt and fresh black pepper, to taste

1 cup (150 g) cherry tomatoes, halved

1 head red-leaf lettuce, torn

1 head romaine lettuce, torn

Make the dressing by using the large holes on a box grater and carefully grating the heirloom tomato into a medium bowl; discard the skin. Add the olive oil, vinegar, lemon juice, mustard and parsley; season with salt and pepper. Whisk well until combined.

Toss the cherry tomatoes and the lettuces together in a large bowl. Add the tomato vinaigrette, a little at a time, until they are dressed as desired.

tip: The closer your tomatoes are to harvest, the less water you should give the fruit for the highest concentration of sugar. Don't withhold water, but don't flood them too often either.

green bean tempura with lemon wasabi mayonnaise

Flatter a passel of green beans by coating them in an airy batter of whipped egg whites, club soda and flour. Serve them hot and crunchy with a smattering of salt and a smear of wasabi-spiked mayonnaise. These do well as an appetizer, a snack, an accompaniment or even a meal unto themselves.

serves 4–6

1 cup (220 g) mayonnaise
2 tsp (10 ml) soy sauce
2 tsp (13 g) wasabi paste
1 tsp lemon juice
4 egg whites
2 cups (250 g) all-purpose flour
2 cups (480 ml) chilled club soda
Vegetable oil, for frying
1½ lbs (680 g) green beans, trimmed
Kosher salt, to taste

In a medium bowl, combine the mayonnaise, soy sauce, wasabi paste and lemon juice; set aside. In a separate large bowl, beat the egg whites until soft peaks form. Whisk in the flour and club soda until the batter just comes together; do not overmix. Use the batter immediately or place it in the refrigerator to keep it cool until ready.

Pour the vegetable oil into a large pot, a few inches deep. Heat it until shimmering, about 350°F (175°C). Working in batches, dip the green beans in the prepared batter, allowing the excess to run off. Fry until the batter is a crisp, light golden brown and the beans are a bright green, 2 to 3 minutes. Transfer them with a slotted spoon to a paper towel–lined plate, and season with salt. Serve with the mayonnaise for dipping.

quick curry pickled cucumbers

While the end of summer has me focused completely on canning and putting up what bounty I can, mid-summer has me reaching for quick pickles left and right. They are excitingly adaptable, and I have yet to find a vegetable that doesn't benefit from a vinegary punch. Here they are with curry powder and turmeric.

makes about 4 pints (306 g) of pickles

2 cups (480 ml) apple cider vinegar

2 tbsp (17 g) kosher salt

1 cup (192 g) granulated sugar

4 large cloves garlic, halved

1 tbsp (6 g) medium curry powder

1 tbsp (6 g) black peppercorns

1 tbsp (5 g) coriander seeds

1 tbsp (11 g) mustard seeds

1 tsp ground turmeric

12 sprigs of fresh dill

2 lbs (907 g) cucumbers, sliced into spears

Bring the vinegar, salt, sugar, garlic, curry powder, peppercorns, coriander seeds, mustard seeds, turmeric and 2 cups (480 ml) of water to a boil in a medium pot over high heat. Reduce the heat to medium-low and simmer for 10 minutes.

Heat resealable jars under hot running water for 1 minute. Dry the jars and pack them full of the dill and cucumbers. Ladle the hot brine over the cucumbers until they're submerged, and allow it to cool to room temperature for 30 minutes.

Cover the jars with their lids, and refrigerate them for at least 2 hours before serving, or up to 3 weeks.

tip: Look up to the sky when growing cucumbers! Think of trellises or other support systems that would allow their vines to climb versus sprawling across the ground. Giving cucumbers vertical support is a proven method for increasing your yields.

tomatillo-strawberry salad

Tomatillos are a slightly sweet and totally tangy garden favorite of mine, and while most often served in Mexican preparations, they thrive particularly well when paired with sweet fruit. In this recipe, each mouthful yields a juicy burst of strawberry coupled with the tart pucker of tomatillo and lime. Enjoy this salad for a picnic or as a refreshment for the hottest of days.

serves 4–6

4 cups (660 g) strawberries, hulled and sliced

½ lb (227 g) tomatillos, husked, quartered and sliced

½ red onion, thinly sliced

2 tbsp (30 ml) fresh lime juice

2 tbsp (30 ml) extra-virgin olive oil

1 tbsp (1 g) chopped fresh cilantro, plus more for serving

¼ tsp kosher salt

⅛ tsp ground coriander

⅔ cup (97 g) feta cheese

Torn fresh mint, for serving

Combine the strawberries, tomatillos and red onion in a large bowl.

In a small bowl, whisk together the lime juice, olive oil, cilantro, salt and coriander.

Pour the vinaigrette on top of the strawberries and tomatillos, and toss well to combine. Top with the feta, mint and cilantro.

fresh tomato sauce

Any fresh tomatoes you have will thrive in this preparation. I have found that seeding the tomatoes does not make a detectable difference in taste, but feel free to add this step if you have a preference. Can or freeze this sauce and enjoy it as often as you can while knee-deep in tomato season. This sauce is great over pasta, in soup, splashed into a curry, as a nest for baked eggs, as a base for ratatouille or as a substitute for other tomato sauces in recipes in this book, including the Whole Eggplant Parmesan (page 127) and Parmesan-Baked Parsnip Gnocchi with Marinara (page 164).

makes about 3 cups (720 ml)

5 lbs (2.3 kg) fresh tomatoes
¼ cup (60 ml) extra-virgin olive oil
3 cloves garlic, minced
1 small onion, finely chopped
1 stalk celery, finely chopped
1 large carrot, grated
Pinch of crushed red pepper
1 tbsp (20 g) tomato paste
¾ tsp kosher salt
1 bay leaf
Fresh basil, for serving

Bring a large pot of water to a boil over high heat. Prepare an ice-water bath in the sink. Slice a small X on the bottom of each tomato, and throw them into the boiling water for about 20 seconds. Transfer them to the water bath to shock them—they will be all the more eager to slip out of their skins. Discard the skins. Coarsely chop the tomatoes, reserving all of their juices. If you prefer to remove the seeds, simply separate them before chopping.

Heat the olive oil in a large pot over medium heat. Add the garlic, onion, celery, carrot and a pinch of crushed red pepper. Sauté the vegetables until they begin to soften, 8 to 10 minutes. Add the tomato paste, stir and cook an additional minute. Add the reserved tomatoes, salt and bay leaf, and bring to a boil. Lower the heat to maintain a gentle simmer, and cook until the sauce has reduced by half, about 30 to 45 minutes. Discard the bay leaf, and adjust the salt as needed. Finish with ribbons of fresh basil.

tip: Tomato varieties are grouped into determinate and indeterminate breeds, the former being varieties that tend to produce a heavy harvest all at once before slowing production. Determinate varieties are good plants for small spaces and containers or for those who wish to can their tomatoes or make paste all at once. Indeterminate varieties grow to be giant plants, requiring much support but also lasting the entirety of the season for all your salad, slicing and sandwich needs.

chipotle tomato jam

Tomato jam is one of many great endeavors when you're faced with a high tide of summer's tomatoes. This sweet, smoky, spicy and totally jammy rendition would be perfect slathered on warm biscuits or enjoyed alongside eggs.

makes about 1 pint (640 g)

2 lbs (907 g) tomatoes, roughly chopped (use any size you like, but I use plums for this recipe)

¾ cup (144 g) granulated sugar

3 tbsp (45 ml) fresh lemon juice

1 tbsp (14 g) freshly grated ginger

2 chipotle chilis in adobo sauce, minced, plus 1 tsp adobo sauce

½ tsp cumin

Combine the tomatoes, sugar, lemon juice, ginger, chilis, adobo sauce and cumin in a large saucepot over medium-high heat, and bring to a boil. Reduce the heat and simmer, stirring occasionally, until the mixture reaches a thick, jam-like consistency, about 1 hour depending on your tomatoes.

Try serving this jam on a grilled cheese sandwich, swirled into a savory soup for a spicy kick or as part of a cheese board.

blistered green beans with green romesco

Make sure the green beans have time to blister in the hot skillet, as this is when you will attain the greatest flavor. Enjoy the well-charred beans with a spoonful of piquant Romesco born from green bell peppers, poblanos and tomatillos. Feel free to take some liberties with the peppers if you have other varieties growing.

serves 4–6

1 small green bell pepper, ribbed, seeded and roughly chopped

1 large poblano chili, stemmed, seeded and roughly chopped

2 tomatillos, roughly chopped

¼ cup (60 ml) plus 3 tbsp (45 ml) extra-virgin olive oil, divided

Kosher salt, to taste

2 cloves garlic

½ cup (60 g) almonds, toasted

1 tsp crushed red pepper

½ cup (8 g) cilantro

1 tsp sherry vinegar

Fresh black pepper, to taste

1½ lbs (680 g) green beans, trimmed

Preheat the oven to 425°F (218°C). Line a large rimmed baking sheet with aluminum foil.

Toss the bell pepper, poblano and tomatillos on the sheet with 1 tablespoon (15 ml) of oil. Season with salt. Roast for 20 minutes, until tender. Cool slightly. Add the garlic to a food processor and chop. Add the toasted almonds and crushed red pepper, and process until a paste forms. Add the pepper mixture to the processor along with the cilantro, vinegar and ¼ cup (60 ml) of olive oil. Season to taste with salt and pepper.

Heat 1 tablespoon (15 ml) of the oil in a large skillet over medium-high heat. Add half of the green beans and cook them, undisturbed, until they begin to blister, about 2 minutes. Toss and continue to cook, tossing often, until they're tender and blistered in spots, 7 to 9 minutes. Remove from the heat and place on a platter. Season with salt and pepper. Repeat with another tablespoon (15 ml) of oil and the remaining beans.

Spoon the green Romesco over the blistered beans, and serve them as a summery appetizer or side dish.

tip: When deciding which green bean varieties to grow, consider the space requirements for pole beans and bush beans. Pole beans require vertical support, whereas bush beans seek horizontal space and are often planted in double rows (6 to 8 inches [15 to 20 cm] apart) to support one another.

peperonata

While simple, this recipe is an intentionally basic preparation that allows the freshest bounty to shine—in this case, sweet summer peppers. A low and slow simmer with fresh garlic, tomatoes, herbs and olive oil allows the peppers to take on an irresistible silkiness, flush with flavor and somewhere between a stew and a relish. Serve this as a side, or spread it generously over grilled crusty bread. Try placing it alongside a frittata or an omelet, tucked into a grilled cheese sandwich or tossed with fresh pasta.

serves 4–6

½ cup (120 ml) extra-virgin olive oil, divided

4 medium cloves garlic, sliced thin

1 medium yellow onion, sliced thin

4 large sweet bell peppers (yellow, orange or red), stemmed, seeded and sliced thin

½ lb (227 g) tomatoes, puréed

1 sprig of fresh basil

1 sprig of fresh oregano

Kosher salt, to taste

1 tbsp (15 ml) red wine vinegar

In a large pot over medium heat, warm ¼ cup (60 ml) of olive oil. Add the garlic and cook, stirring often, until it turns golden. Add the onion, and increase the heat to medium-high. Cook, stirring, an additional 2 minutes. Add the peppers and cook, stirring occasionally, until they begin to soften, 20 minutes.

Stir in the puréed tomatoes along with the basil and oregano sprigs. Bring to a boil and then reduce the heat to maintain a gentle simmer. Cook, stirring occasionally, until the peppers and onion have completely softened, 45 minutes to 1 hour. Stir in the remaining olive oil and season to taste with salt. Discard the basil and oregano. Stir in the vinegar, and serve at room temperature. Preserve the peperonata in the refrigerator for about a week by jarring and covering it with a layer of olive oil.

cherry tomato confit with shallot & garlic

A good portion of the growing season is spent embracing the many options available for preserving the harvest. A rich and slow-cooked confit is a forever-lauded choice. Much like the peppers in peperonata, the olive oil–bathed tomatoes dissolve tenderly into a delicate and delightful condiment. I find myself soaking this up with bread as often as I have it, though it rarely sticks around.

makes 4 cups (960 g)

2 pints (600 g) cherry tomatoes

12 cloves garlic, peeled and smashed

6 small shallots, peeled and halved

8 sprigs of fresh thyme

½ cup (20 g) fresh basil leaves

2 cups (480 ml) extra-virgin olive oil

1 tsp kosher salt

Pinch of crushed red pepper

Preheat the oven to 300°F (150°C).

Add the tomatoes, garlic, shallots, thyme and basil to a deep baking dish. Add the olive oil, making sure everything is submerged. Sprinkle with kosher salt and crushed red pepper.

Cook, uncovered, for 2 to 3 hours, until the tomatoes are swollen, their skins wrinkled, and the garlic and shallots are tender. Allow to cool, and store in the refrigerator in an airtight container for up to 2 weeks. Bring it back to room temperature before serving. Alternatively, you may freeze the tomatoes for up to 2 months.

Try enjoying this confit as part of a larger meal by using it to top pizza, spooning it over your favorite pasta with olives and capers, drizzling it over a salad or including it as an add-in for the Roasted Tomato Risotto (page 120).

lemony zucchini coins with brown butter bread crumbs

A smaller, young zucchini works best here so that you may slice it into uniform coins. Tossing the seared zucchini with garlic and lemon offers a delectable outfit for your summer squash. Finish this side with a sprinkling of toasted bread crumbs richly flavored with browned butter.

serves 4

2 tbsp (30 ml) extra-virgin olive oil

2 large cloves garlic, sliced thin

1½ lbs (680 g) small zucchini, sliced into ¼" (6-mm) coins

2 tsp (4 g) freshly grated lemon zest, divided

Kosher salt and fresh black pepper, to taste

2 tbsp (28 g) unsalted butter

3 tbsp (12 g) fresh bread crumbs

Heat the olive oil in a large skillet over medium-high heat. Add the garlic and cook, stirring, until it's fragrant and golden, 2 to 3 minutes. Add the zucchini and 1 teaspoon of lemon zest and cook over high heat, shaking the skillet to toss the coins until they're colored on both sides. Season with salt and pepper.

Meanwhile, melt the butter in a small skillet over medium heat. Continue cooking it until it begins to brown and smell toasted, 3 minutes. Add the bread crumbs and cook, stirring, until they are golden and toasted. Mix in the remaining 1 teaspoon of lemon zest, and season gently with salt and pepper. Add the bread crumbs to the zucchini, toss and serve hot.

on-hand hot sauce

This is an excellent number for whatever spicy pepper varieties you have bursting at summer's seams, although the most striking sauce is made by using a single variety. Homemade hot sauce is flavorful and easy to achieve at home; the perfect candidate for a simple weekend project. The longer you allow it to ferment, the greater the depth of flavor.

makes about 2½ cups (600 ml)

1 lb (454 g) stemmed fresh chilis
4 large cloves garlic, peeled
2 tbsp (17 g) kosher salt
1 cup (240 ml) distilled white vinegar
½ cup (120 ml) fresh lime juice
1 tbsp (12 g) granulated sugar

In a food processor or blender, pulse the chilis together with the garlic and salt to form a coarse purée. Transfer this mixture to a 1-quart (1-L) glass jar, and cover it with a piece of cheesecloth secured with a rubber band. Set the jar on the counter, and allow it to ferment at room temperature for a day.

Transfer the chilis to a blender, add the vinegar, lime juice and sugar and process until completely smooth. Transfer the mixture to a new jar, cover it with a cheesecloth and allow it to ferment at room temperature for a minimum of an additional day and up to a week.

Purée the mixture once more in a blender until smooth. Strain it through a fine-mesh sieve into a jar or glass bottle, and keep it refrigerated. Separation is natural; give it a good shake before using. The sauce will keep for at least a month.

tip: As your peppers begin to fruit and near the point of maturity, try watering them sparingly. Withholding water increases the level of capsicum, resulting in a delectably spicy harvest.

open-faced tomato sandwich with rosemary-marinated feta

The feta here is herb-forward and bright. Try to begin the marinade ahead of time, as the longer the feta sits, the more it can soak in the rich and fruity olive oil. Having a jar of it on hand is akin to kitchen gold in the heat of the summer. Buy or bake a good loaf of bread and toast or grill it well. Top it with layered slabs of marinated feta and your freshest slices of tomatoes, and enjoy this simple, but very necessary, sandwich often.

serves 4

8 oz (227 g) feta, sliced ½" (1 cm) thick

4 sprigs of fresh rosemary

4 sprigs of fresh thyme

4 sprigs of fresh oregano

2 bay leaves

2 dried red chilis, crushed

2 tbsp (30 ml) fresh lemon juice

1 cup (240 ml) extra-virgin olive oil

4 thick slices of bread, for serving

4 tomato slices, for serving

Flaky sea salt, such as Maldon, for serving

Fresh black pepper, for serving

Stack the slices of feta in a medium jar. Layer them with the rosemary, thyme, oregano, bay leaves and chilis. Add the lemon juice, and cover everything with the olive oil. Refrigerate for at least 1 hour and up to a week.

Toast slices of bread in a 375°F (190°C) oven until golden. Smear the marinated feta onto the bread, or top it with whole slabs of feta. Add the tomato slices, and drizzle them with marinade oil. Finish with a dusting of salt and pepper.

tip: If you're using seedlings or starts for your tomato garden, make sure to plant them deeply. Snip off the lowest branches and leaves, and bury the leafless part in its entirety. Whatever stem you bury will sprout additional roots, making your plants that much stronger.

grilled pizza with herby pesto

Pizza is the best cue we could ever take for a garden dinner, and I find it effortlessly adaptable to every season, summer being no exception. While I recommend topping it with fresh tomatoes and corn here, think of this recipe as a map and use what is fresh and available. If you've never grilled pizza, now is the time! This softly sweet dough easily comes together in a matter of hours and sears perfectly on a hot grill.

makes 2 small or 1 large pizza

pizza dough

2 cups (275 g) bread flour, plus more for dusting

1 cup (125 g) whole-wheat flour

2¼ tsp (9 g) instant yeast

2 tsp (6 g) kosher salt

1 tsp granulated sugar

1 tsp honey

1½ cups (360 ml) lukewarm water (about 110°F [43°C])

2½ tbsp (38 ml) extra-virgin olive oil, divided, plus more for brushing

herby pesto

1 cup (40 g) fresh basil leaves, plus more for serving

½ cup (20 g) fresh chives, roughly chopped

⅓ cup (40 g) pine nuts, toasted

½ cup (50 g) freshly grated Parmesan

¼ cup (10 g) fresh parsley

¼ cup (10 g) fresh tarragon leaves

2 cloves garlic, peeled

⅓ cup (80 ml) extra-virgin olive oil, plus more for serving

Kosher salt and fresh black pepper, to taste

2 pints (600 g) cherry tomatoes, halved

3 fresh ears corn, shucked

Mozzarella, torn

In the bowl of a stand mixer, combine the bread flour, whole-wheat flour, yeast, salt and sugar, stirring them together to incorporate. With the mixer running, add the honey, water and 2 tablespoons (30 ml) of olive oil, and mix until the dough forms a ball. Adjust the consistency of the dough as needed. If the dough appears too sticky, adjust it with additional flour; if it's too dry, add additional water 1 tablespoon (15 ml) at a time.

Dust a surface with additional flour, scrape the dough out and knead it together for 1 to 2 minutes into a smooth, firm ball.

Coat the inside of a large bowl with ½ tablespoon (8 ml) of olive oil. Add the dough, cover it with plastic wrap and let it rise for 1 to 2 hours until it has doubled.

Meanwhile, heat your grill for medium-high, direct heat.

Make the pesto by combining the basil, chives, pine nuts, Parmesan, parsley, tarragon, garlic and olive oil together in a food processor. Process until smooth; season to taste with salt and pepper.

Turn the dough out onto a lightly floured surface, and gently deflate it with the palm of your hand. Divide the dough into two equal pieces, cover them with a lightly floured kitchen towel and let them rest for 10 minutes. Working with one round at a time, use your hands to gently stretch the dough outwards until a thin (but not paper-thin) crust is achieved. The dough does not have to be round. Repeat with the remaining dough. Brush with olive oil.

Working with both pizzas, place them oil side down onto the grill and cook for 1 to 2 minutes until they're lightly browned beneath yet soft on top. While cooking, brush the top sides with additional olive oil.

Once lightly browned, remove the pizzas from the grill, and place them, cooked side up, onto a large cookie sheet. Coat the pizzas with generous amounts of pesto, tomatoes, corn and mozzarella. Return the pizzas to the grill and cook, lid down, until the undersides and edges are browned and the cheese has melted. Finish with fresh basil and a drizzle of olive oil.

tomato cobbler with gruyère-chive biscuits

This savory cobbler makes a fine case for an easy summer dinner. While I've used cherry tomatoes here, feel free to substitute with grape or plum tomatoes. The beauty is being able to use what's available and transforming the flavors. The filling is ripe with savory and sweet flavor, lent effortlessly by tomatoes, herbs, garlic and fennel. The biscuit topping comes together easily and is punctuated by fresh chives and nutty Gruyère cheese. Serve this hot with a fresh dinner salad composed of tender baby greens.

serves 6–8

filling

¼ cup (60 ml) extra-virgin olive oil

2 medium onions, diced

½ fennel bulb, finely diced

Pinch of kosher salt

2 cloves garlic, minced

1 tsp chopped fresh thyme

½ tsp crushed red pepper

2 lbs (907 g) cherry tomatoes, divided

1 tsp light brown sugar

2 tbsp (16 g) all-purpose flour

topping

1½ cups (188 g) all-purpose flour

1½ tsp (7 g) baking powder

¼ tsp baking soda

½ tsp kosher salt

6 tbsp (84 g) cold unsalted butter, cut into small pieces

1 tsp finely minced chives

1 cup (110 g) grated Gruyère cheese

⅔ cup (160 ml) buttermilk, plus more for brushing

Flaky salt, such as Maldon, for sprinkling

Preheat the oven to 375°F (190°C).

To make the filling, heat the olive oil in a large skillet over medium-high heat. Add the onions and fennel with a pinch of salt, and cook, stirring occasionally, until softened and golden, 5 to 7 minutes. Add the garlic, thyme and crushed red pepper, and cook for an additional minute. Add half of the cherry tomatoes and the brown sugar. Cook, stirring occasionally, until the tomatoes just begin to soften. Remove from the heat, and fold in the remaining tomatoes and the flour.

To make the topping, whisk the flour, baking powder, baking soda and salt together in a large bowl. Add the butter, and use a pastry cutter or your fingers to rub the mixture together until small clumps the size of peas form. Add the minced chives and Gruyère. Add the buttermilk, and gently mix with a fork until a sticky dough just forms.

Transfer the tomato mixture into a 2-quart (2-L) baking dish. Spoon the biscuit dough over the tomato filling, leaving spaces for the tomatoes to steam through. Brush the dough with additional buttermilk. Lightly sprinkle the biscuits with a few flakes of salt. Bake until golden and bubbling, 50 to 60 minutes. Allow the cobbler to rest for 15 to 20 minutes before serving.

spicy summer soba salad

Nutty buckwheat noodles thrive in cold preparations, making this salad perfect for picnics or a weekend at the lake. Look to involve the garden's sturdier occupants; ones that can benefit from time spent marinating, such as red cabbage, carrots and scallions. The union of sesame, lime and Sriracha in the dressing makes for an indulgent and absurdly addicting combination.

serves 4–6

⅓ cup (80 ml) unseasoned rice vinegar

⅓ cup (80 ml) grapeseed oil

2 tbsp (30 ml) fresh lime juice

1 tbsp (15 ml) Sriracha

1 tbsp (15 ml) toasted sesame oil

6 oz (170 g) soba noodles

1 cup (118 g) edamame

1 cup (70 g) shredded red cabbage

1 cup (125 g) finely julienned carrots

1 cup (115 g) finely julienned cucumber

½ cup (50 g) chopped fresh scallions

Cilantro and sesame seeds, for garnish

In a medium bowl, whisk together the rice vinegar, grapeseed oil, lime juice, Sriracha and sesame oil.

In a large pot of salted boiling water, cook the soba noodles until al dente, about 5 minutes. Add the edamame for the last minute, just to warm it. Drain the soba and edamame, and rinse them under cold running water until cooled. Shake off any excess water. Transfer them to a large bowl and toss them with the prepared dressing. Add the red cabbage, carrots, cucumber and scallions and toss again. Serve either refrigerated or at room temperature and garnish with cilantro and sesame seeds.

stuffed poblanos with farro & pinto beans

With any luck, high summer brings abundance. Whenever I find myself faced with a flush of peppers, I turn to stuffing them as a great vegetarian dinner option—here with farro and pinto beans. I boost the heat with a serrano-spiked salsa and pepper jack cheese, but feel free to omit these for a milder preparation.

serves 6

1 cup (200 g) farro

1 lb (454 g) tomatillos, husked and rinsed

½ large yellow onion, peeled

1 serrano pepper

2 large cloves garlic, peeled

½ cup (8 g) loosely packed cilantro leaves and tender stems, chopped

Kosher salt, to taste

1 (15-oz [425-g]) can pinto beans, drained and rinsed

1 cup (120 g) shredded pepper jack cheese, divided

1 tsp cumin

4 large poblano peppers, halved lengthwise and seeded

Preheat the broiler in your oven.

Rinse and drain the farro. Add it to a medium pot and cover it with about 1 quart (1 L) of water. Bring to a boil; reduce the heat to medium-low, and simmer for 25 to 30 minutes until tender. Drain off the excess water.

While the farro is boiling, line a baking sheet with aluminum foil, and add the tomatillos, onion and serrano. Broil until they begin to char, about 8 minutes. Carefully add the garlic, and broil an additional 2 minutes. Remove the baking sheet, and preheat the oven to 425°F (218°C).

Stem the serrano, and add it to a blender along with the tomatillos, onion, garlic and cilantro. Pulse the blender a few times to create a semismooth salsa; season to taste with salt.

In a large bowl, combine the farro, half of the prepared tomatillo salsa, the pinto beans, ½ cup (60 g) of pepper jack cheese and the cumin; season to taste with additional salt.

Divide the farro and bean stuffing between the poblano halves, placing each in a large baking dish. Sprinkle the tops of the poblanos with the remaining cheese, and cover the top of the baking dish tightly with aluminum foil.

Bake the poblanos until tender, about 45 minutes. Uncover, and continue to cook until the cheese has browned, an additional 10 minutes. Allow the peppers to cool for 10 minutes before serving them topped with the remaining tomatillo salsa.

cucumber-pear soda with ginger & mint

Cucumber easily lends itself to a refreshing drink because of its high water content. Pack some in a blender with juicy pears, sweet mint, tart lime juice and sharp ginger for a delicious fusion. Pour it into cold, ice-filled glasses and top it off with sparkling water for an ultrahydrating sip on a hot day.

serves 4

2 large pears (about 2 lbs [907 g]), roughly chopped

1 cucumber, peeled and roughly chopped

⅓ cup (13 g) packed fresh mint leaves, plus more for serving

1" (3-cm) piece of ginger, grated

¼ cup (60 ml) fresh lime juice

Ice, for serving

Sparkling water, for serving

Combine the pears, cucumber, mint, ginger and ¾ cup (180 ml) of water in a blender, and purée until smooth. Strain the mixture through a fine-mesh sieve into a large bowl. Add the lime juice, and chill in the refrigerator for at least 1 hour.

Serve chilled over ice and topped with the sparkling water and mint leaves for garnish.

lemon–poppy seed zucchini loaf cake

There's often a point in the season when many people realize just how prolific a zucchini plant can be. When you begin to take inventory and are unsure of what to do with your bounty, might I suggest this sweet lemon–poppy seed loaf? The zucchini contributes a lovely moisture to this poppy seed–speckled lemon cake, making it perfect for breakfast or snacking in the late afternoon.

makes 1 (8½ × 4½" [22 × 11–cm]) loaf

1½ cups (188 g) all-purpose flour, plus more for dusting

2 tsp (8 g) baking powder

½ tsp kosher salt, plus 1 pinch

1 tbsp (6 g) grated lemon zest

¾ cup (144 g) granulated sugar

2 large eggs, at room temperature

½ cup (120 ml) vegetable oil

1 tsp vanilla extract

6 tbsp (90 ml) fresh lemon juice, divided

1 cup (125 g) zucchini, grated

1 tbsp (8 g) poppy seeds, plus more for sprinkling

1 cup (130 g) confectioners' sugar

Preheat the oven to 350°F (175°C). Lightly coat an 8½ × 4½–inch (22 × 11–cm) loaf pan with nonstick spray and a dusting of flour, shaking out to release any excess.

In a medium bowl, whisk together the flour, baking powder and salt.

In a large bowl, using your hands, massage the lemon zest into the sugar until the mixture becomes fragrant and resembles wet sand. Add the eggs, vegetable oil and vanilla, and beat until light and thick, about 3 minutes.

Add the dry ingredients into the liquid ingredients, followed by 3 tablespoons (45 ml) of lemon juice, stirring or beating gently until smooth. Fold in the zucchini and poppy seeds. Scoop the batter into the prepared pan.

Bake the loaf for 50 to 60 minutes, or until golden brown and a toothpick inserted into the center returns clean.

Remove the loaf from the oven, and cool it in the pan for 10 minutes.

Meanwhile, make the glaze by dissolving the confectioners' sugar in the remaining 3 tablespoons (45 ml) of lemon juice. Add a pinch of salt.

Turn the loaf out onto a wire rack. Pierce the top in several places with a knife and pour the glaze over the cake. Sprinkle it with additional poppy seeds and allow it to sit until the glaze is set, about 30 minutes.

Store in an airtight container at room temperature, or freeze for longer storage.

tip: One squash plant alone is prolific enough to feed you for an entire season. For the sweetest flavor, harvest when it's young and tender—no longer than 6 inches (15 cm) for elongated varieties, or 4 inches (10 cm) across for wide ones. Perhaps you are familiar with the moment when you've seemingly turned your back for only a second, only to find your zucchini has tripled in size. Try using these leviathans for baking and making relish.

blackberry-corn crisp

Freshly picked corn's natural sugar content makes it an enthusiastic element for desserts. Find one example here: the corn studded in the cornmeal topping of an oven-warmed crisp bursting with lively sweet-tart blackberries and lime. As an end to a summer's eve dinner, serve this dolloped with a scoop of vanilla ice cream—easy to assemble and even easier to enjoy.

serves 6

4 cups (576 g) fresh blackberries

1 tbsp (10 g) cornstarch

½ cup (96 g) granulated sugar

1 tsp finely grated lime zest

Juice of ½ lime

¾ cup (94 g) flour

½ cup (85 g) cornmeal

½ cup (110 g) packed light brown sugar

Pinch of kosher salt

½ cup (115 g) chilled unsalted butter, cut into pieces

1 cup (144 g) fresh corn kernels (from about 2 average ears)

Preheat the oven to 375°F (190°C).

In a shallow 2-quart (2-L) baking dish, combine the blackberries, cornstarch, sugar, lime zest and lime juice.

In a medium bowl, whisk the flour with the cornmeal, brown sugar and a pinch of salt. Add the butter to the bowl, and work it into the flour until the mixture is no longer sandy and is beginning to stick and clump together. Add the corn kernels. Distribute the topping over the blackberries.

Bake the crisp until the topping is golden and the berries are thick and bubbling, 60 minutes. Remove and cool the crisp on a wire rack for 30 minutes before serving.

autumn

The onset of autumn is a moment in time deeply fortified and ripe with plenitude. The very end of summer begins to bleed into the shifting atmosphere, destined to trade the heat for a migration to cooler temperatures. Yet it's by this interim that I will forever be transfixed. Autumn is quick to humble any of my residual hastiness; it is a patient reminder that the sultry swell of summer is determinate but that the garden is not.

The cool nights beckon for a different kind of fare that radiates nourishment, comfort and warmth. My favorites include the deeply savory Roasted Tomato Risotto (page 120), the humble and homey Beans & Greens (page 124), an ultra-satisfying eggplant Parmesan made out of the entire eggplant (page 127) and perhaps one of the sweetest twists ever, Butternut Squash Ice Cream with Coconut and Lemongrass (page 135).

ginger-roasted carrots with carrot-top gremolata

Sweet carrots are roasted with sharp and spicy garlic and ginger, teasing out and complementing their intrinsic sweetness. Save the carrot tops: they're completely edible! Chop them finely and toss them with cilantro, lime zest and roasted peanuts for a tasty topping.

serves 4

1 lb (454 g) medium carrots with tops, tops reserved

4 large cloves garlic, peeled and smashed

4 ¼" (6-mm) slices fresh ginger

1 tbsp (15 ml) extra-virgin olive oil

1 tbsp (14 g) unsalted butter

Kosher salt and fresh black pepper, to taste

¼ cup (4 g) fresh cilantro, chopped

½ tsp finely grated lime zest

¼ cup (30 g) dry-roasted peanuts, finely chopped

Preheat the oven to 400°F (200°C).

In a medium baking dish, combine the carrots with ¼ cup (60 ml) of water, garlic, ginger, olive oil and butter; season with salt and pepper. Cover the dish with foil, and roast for 25 to 30 minutes until the carrots are just beginning to become tender. Remove the foil, and roast for an additional 30 minutes until the water has evaporated and the carrots are golden in spots.

For the gremolata, combine the cilantro, lime zest and peanuts in a small bowl. Finely chop the carrot tops until you have ¼ cup (10 g), and add them to the bowl.

Serve the carrots and garlic on a platter and sprinkled with the gremolata.

tip: Carrot seeds take some time to germinate, so do not fret if you don't observe the seedlings sprouting right away. Plant some radish seeds with the carrot seeds; they're quicker to sprout and will remind you of your rows.

coconut milk–braised collard greens

At first appearance, collards may seem large and leathery, but they respond well to a long braise. Cut away the tough inner ribs, and then simply roll the leaves up and slice them into ribbons. Cooked low and slowly, the leaves become pleasantly tender and willingly soak up this rich and creamy coconut milk spiced with garlic, ginger, chili and lime. Sweet, spicy and sour, this is a favorite braise for a beloved green. Serve it as a side dish or an accompaniment to a larger meal. It would pair well with a frittata, a bowl of rice and beans or a curry.

serves 4–6

1 tbsp (14 g) coconut oil

1 tbsp (15 ml) toasted sesame oil

1 large onion, chopped

3 cloves garlic, minced

1 Fresno chili, seeded and minced

1 tsp grated fresh ginger

2 lbs (907 g) collard greens, stemmed and leaves coarsely chopped

1 (12-oz [340-g]) can unsweetened coconut milk

½ cup (120 ml) vegetable stock

Juice from 1 lime

Kosher salt and fresh black pepper, to taste

Sesame seeds, for serving

Melt the coconut oil and sesame oil together in a large pot over medium-high heat. Add the onion, garlic, chili and ginger, and sauté until tender and fragrant, 6 minutes. Add the greens, and sauté until they begin to wilt, 2 minutes. Add the coconut milk and vegetable stock, and bring to a boil. Reduce the heat, cover and simmer, stirring occasionally, until the greens are very tender, 40 minutes. Stir in the lime juice, and season with salt and pepper. Serve the greens topped with sesame seeds.

blackened red cabbage with lemon-caraway butter

Red cabbage can often get lost in the shuffle of more "exciting" vegetable options—but it is not to be misplaced or forgotten. Slice a small head in half and sear in its signature nutty sweetness. Baste it the rest of the way with a lemon and caraway–spiced butter, a vividly savory companion, and finish it with a dash of vinegar for a sapid cool-weather side. Try serving this roasted cabbage on top of a salad or perhaps as a side to the Swiss Chard Tacos with Chili-Lime Pepitas and Queso Fresco (page 132).

serves 2

¼ cup (56 g) unsalted butter, softened

1 tbsp (7 g) caraway seeds

2 tsp (10 ml) fresh lemon juice

½ tsp kosher salt, plus more for serving

1 tbsp (15 ml) extra-virgin olive oil

½ small red cabbage

2 tsp (10 ml) apple cider vinegar

In a medium bowl, combine the softened butter with the caraway seeds, lemon juice and ½ teaspoon of salt until well blended.

Heat the oil in a large skillet over medium-high heat, and add the cabbage, cut side down. Cook, undisturbed, until the underside is charred, 10 to 15 minutes. Reduce the heat to medium-low, and add the infused butter. Once the butter begins to foam, tilt the skillet toward you, and spoon some butter over the top of the cabbage.

Baste the cabbage every 3 to 4 minutes, adding more butter if necessary. Cook an additional 10 to 15 minutes until the cabbage is knife-tender.

Transfer the cabbage to a cutting board and halve it once more so that you are left with two quarters. Drizzle with the vinegar, season with salt and serve warm.

tuscan kale chips

Transform long, slender kale leaves into an addictive (and timeless) snack. The low oven temperature allows them time to crisp evenly. Feel free to experiment with alternate flavor profiles, herbs or spices—but a finishing of flaky salt is always a surefire way to please the senses.

serves 4

2 large bunches of lacinato kale (also known as Tuscan or dinosaur kale), stemmed and halved crosswise

2 tbsp (30 ml) extra-virgin olive oil

1 tbsp (3 g) chopped fresh rosemary

1 tbsp (3 g) chopped fresh thyme

Smoked salt and fresh black pepper, to taste

Preheat the oven to 300°F (150°C).

In a large bowl, toss the leaves of kale with the oil, massaging it in. Add the rosemary, thyme and a seasoning of smoked salt and pepper. Splay the leaves out on two large rimmed baking sheets and bake the leaves until crisp, 30 minutes.

These are best when fresh, so enjoy them right from the oven.

ember-roasted beets & their greens with calabrian chili aioli

Take advantage of the entire beet, which is completely edible, by cooking both the leafy greens and the root. This is a fine dish to prepare if you're already grilling, as the beets can be nestled right into the embers to char, leaving you with a rich and smoky flesh. Cut away the charred skins to reveal the tender and earthy insides, complemented by a richly smoky and spicy aioli made from Italian Calabrian chilis. Find these chilis tucked in with the Italian goods in your grocery store.

serves 4

2 bunches of medium beets, greens attached

3 cloves garlic, minced

¼ tsp kosher salt

½ cup (110 g) mayonnaise

2 tbsp (30 ml) extra-virgin olive oil

1 tbsp (15 ml) fresh lemon juice

2 tbsp (22 g) chopped, drained, oil-packed Calabrian chilis

Prepare a charcoal grill for medium-high heat.

Cut the greens off of the beets, leaving some stalk attached. Wash the beet greens; reserve.

Allow your grill to burn long enough to produce ash-covered coals, about 15 to 30 minutes. Lightly knock the grill to dust off any accumulated ash, and lay the beets a few inches away from the coals. Cook the beets, occasionally turning them, until they are knife-tender, about 30 to 40 minutes. Remove them from the coals to cool. When the beets are cool enough to handle, peel off the skins. Trim any remaining root and stalk. Cut the beets into wedges or medium slices.

Meanwhile, bring a large pot of salted water to a boil over medium-high heat. Cook the reserved beet greens until tender, about 5 minutes. Drain, squeezing out the excess water, and put them in a bowl.

Make the aioli by putting the garlic and salt into a medium bowl. Mash them together until a paste forms. Whisk in the mayonnaise, olive oil, lemon juice and chilis.

Spoon the aioli onto a platter, and top it with the roasted beets and their greens.

brussels sprouts salad with candied walnuts & pears

Brussels sprouts, among other humble vegetables, are seeing a bit of a renaissance in our modern day. I like to pay homage to them raw, in a fresh salad, bolstered by a welcome cast of candied walnuts, sweet pears, nutty Parmesan, herbs and spicy horseradish—contrasting but coherent elements that keep every bite interesting.

serves 4–6

1 cup (120 g) walnut halves

2 tbsp (28 g) brown sugar

½ tsp ground cinnamon

¼ tsp kosher salt, plus more for additional seasoning

1 lb (454 g) Brussels sprouts, trimmed, halved lengthwise and thinly sliced crosswise

1 tbsp (15 ml) fresh lemon juice

½ cup (40 g) shaved Parmesan cheese

Fresh black pepper, to taste

1 crisp pear, quartered lengthwise and sliced crosswise

¼ cup (10 g) fresh mint leaves, torn

¼ cup (10 g) flat-leaf parsley, chopped

¼ cup (60 ml) extra-virgin olive oil

Horseradish root, for grating

Preheat the oven to 400°F (200°C). Line a small baking sheet with parchment paper.

Toss the walnut halves with 4 teaspoons (20 ml) of water in a bowl. Add the brown sugar, cinnamon and ¼ teaspoon of salt and toss to coat. Transfer the walnuts to the baking sheet and bake until they are starting to brown, 6 to 8 minutes. Cool until the sugar hardens.

Meanwhile, in a large serving bowl, toss the Brussels sprouts with the lemon juice and Parmesan. Season with salt and pepper. Add the candied walnuts and pear. Add the mint, parsley and olive oil, and toss to combine. Season to taste with additional salt and pepper if needed. Serve topped with grated horseradish.

tip: Truly, Brussels sprouts are one of the best members of a fall garden. Often, I've found myself harvesting these tiny cabbages right in time for the Thanksgiving holiday. Be sure to delay their transplanting to July or August to give them enough time to mature beneath cooler temperatures. Ideally, you'd harvest them past your first frost. Harvest them tender, when they are about 1 inch (3 cm) in diameter. Make great use of their leaves: they are completely edible, and I often treat them as you would a collard leaf wrap.

coriander-roasted broccoli with ginger-miso yogurt

Roasted broccoli is a dish I prepare weekly, as well as one that I find myself often craving. Try this rather addictive iteration, with broccoli spiced with cumin and coriander, charred to perfection in the oven's heat and cooled with a ginger-and-miso yogurt dip. Try serving this as part of a snack platter, or perhaps as a side to the Baked Falafel with Pickled Onions and Lemon Tahini Sauce (page 45).

serves 4

1 tbsp (5 g) coriander seeds

¼ tsp cumin seeds

1 clove garlic, halved

Pinch of kosher salt

¼ cup (60 ml) olive oil

2 large heads broccoli (about 2 lb [907 g]), cut into florets

1 tbsp (17 g) low-sodium white miso

1 tbsp (15 ml) unseasoned rice vinegar

1 tbsp (15 ml) fresh lime juice

½ tsp grated fresh ginger

2 large cloves garlic, minced

2 tbsp (30 ml) sesame oil

2 tbsp (30 ml) grapeseed oil

2 tbsp (30 g) plain Greek yogurt

Preheat the oven to 450°F (232°C).

Grind or crush the coriander and cumin seeds until fine. Combine the coriander, cumin, halved garlic, a pinch of salt and the olive oil in a food processor, and purée until smooth. Remove the dressing to a small bowl.

Splay the broccoli out onto two large rimmed baking sheets, and toss with the coriander oil. Roast until tender and beginning to brown in spots, 15 to 20 minutes.

Meanwhile, combine the miso, vinegar, lime juice, ginger, minced garlic, sesame oil, grapeseed oil and yogurt in a food processor, and process until smooth.

Serve the roasted broccoli with the ginger-miso yogurt.

butternut squash maple butter

Give your cool-season squash varieties a roast in the oven, and then blend them with sweet maple syrup and spices to mirror the deeply satisfying experience of apple butter. Enjoy this butter spread thickly on toast, spooned into plain yogurt or as an addition to your next baked quick bread.

makes about 1 cup (230 g)

1 (1–1½ lb [454–680 g]) butternut squash

1 tbsp (14 g) butter, cut into small pieces

⅓ cup (80 ml) pure maple syrup

2 tsp (10 ml) fresh lemon juice

Pinches of ground cinnamon

Pinches of clove

Preheat the oven to 400°F (200°C).

Trim both ends of the squash and halve it lengthwise, discarding the seeds. Transfer the squash, cut side up, to an aluminum foil–lined baking sheet. Dot each half with pieces of butter, cover with aluminum foil and roast until softened, 40 minutes to 1 hour. Remove from the heat and let cool. Scoop the flesh when the squash is cool enough to handle.

Purée the squash with the maple syrup in a food processor or blender until smooth. Add the squash mixture to a small pot with a splash of water, the lemon juice and a couple pinches of ground cinnamon and clove. Simmer, stirring often, until the mixture is thick and warm. Cool and store in the refrigerator for up to a week.

baked sweet potato wedges with maple-chipotle mayonnaise

Roasting sweet potatoes plays well with the sweetness we have come to cherish them for. These wedges remain a bit irresistible to me with their crisp edges and creamy insides. Dip them in a sweet, smoky and spicy mayonnaise for a side to heartier fare, such as a veggie burger. These wedges also make for the perfect delicious snack: try serving them alongside the Coriander-Roasted Broccoli with Ginger-Miso Yogurt (page 115).

serves 4–6

4 sweet potatoes, scrubbed and cut lengthwise into wedges

3 tbsp (45 ml) extra-virgin olive oil

Kosher salt and fresh black pepper, to taste

½ cup (110 g) mayonnaise

1 tbsp (15 ml) pure maple syrup

1 tbsp (11 g) minced chipotle chili in adobo sauce, plus ½ tsp adobo sauce

½ tsp Dijon mustard

Preheat the oven to 450°F (232°C).

Toss the sweet potatoes with the olive oil and spread them in an even layer on a large foil-lined, rimmed baking sheet; season with salt and pepper. Roast the potatoes, stirring occasionally, until crisp and tender, 25 to 30 minutes.

Meanwhile, whisk together the mayonnaise, maple syrup, chipotle chili, adobo sauce and Dijon mustard.

Season the hot wedges with extra salt and serve them with a side of the mayonnaise.

tip: Have you ever grown sweet potatoes? If not, don't be intimidated! Sweet potatoes grow well in the heat and offer generous yields, and their pretty foliage is also completely edible. Just be sure to save enough room for them to span out: plant them about 18 inches (46 cm) apart in rows that are 3 feet (91 cm) apart. Immediately following harvest, sweet potatoes are not at their sweetest—they benefit from being left to cure for a period, about a week, during which they will grow to be much sweeter.

roasted tomato risotto

An extra amount of time is required for this risotto, yet it's spent wisely, tempting out and deepening the flavors of summer's tomatoes. The rich and roasted tomatoes blended into the vegetable stock evoke both comfort and familiarity. Serve it in warmed bowls, showered with a healthy sprinkling of Parmesan cheese.

serves 4

1 lb (454 g) Roma tomatoes (or other plum tomatoes)

2 tbsp (30 ml) extra-virgin olive oil, divided

3 large cloves garlic, thinly sliced

6 sprigs of fresh thyme

2½ cups (600 ml) vegetable stock

1 medium onion, finely diced

1 cup (200 g) arborio rice

½ cup (120 ml) dry white wine

Freshly grated Parmesan cheese, for serving

Preheat the oven to 350°F (175°C).

Cut the tomatoes in half lengthwise. Place them, cut side up, on a foil-lined baking sheet. Using 1 tablespoon (15 ml) of olive oil, brush each tomato half. Top each half with a few slivers of garlic and pieces of thyme. Roast the tomatoes for 40 minutes. Once they're finished roasting, discard the thyme.

Blend the tomatoes and garlic with the vegetable stock until smooth. This should yield 3½ cups (830 ml) of liquid total. Bring the blended tomato stock to a simmer in a medium saucepan, and continue to maintain a bare simmer over low heat.

Meanwhile, place a medium saucepan over medium heat, and warm the remaining 1 tablespoon (15 ml) of olive oil. Add the diced onion, and sauté until softened. Add the arborio rice, and cook for 1 minute, stirring to coat it in the olive oil.

Add the white wine to the rice, and cook until it's completely absorbed. Over medium-low heat, begin to add the warmed tomato stock, ½ cup (120 ml) at a time, stirring in and adding more as it's absorbed, 20 to 25 minutes. The risotto is done when the rice has become just tender and taken on a creaminess.

Serve in warmed bowls with Parmesan cheese.

tip: I consider tomatoes as just as much an early fall crop as a late summer one. Often, this time of year produces the very best that tomatoes have to offer. Gardening is many parts intuition, leaving much of the outcome up to the trends in the weather. I have seen many tomato plants produce well into November.

swiss chard gratin

With the onset of colder temperatures, I find myself turning more to the warmth of the oven, and this savory gratin does not disappoint. If you're facing a generous harvest of Swiss chard or other greens, I recommend trying them baked into a luxurious, cheesy, spiced béchamel sauce. Dust the top with lemony, spicy, crispy bread crumbs to finish the dish.

serves 6–8

2 bunches of Swiss chard, about 1 lb (454 g), stemmed and greens sliced

1 cup (60 g) fresh coarse bread crumbs

¼ cup (60 ml) extra-virgin olive oil, divided

1 tsp chopped fresh thyme

1 tsp finely grated lemon zest

½ tsp crushed red pepper

1 cup (100 g) finely grated Parmesan cheese, divided

Kosher salt and fresh black pepper, to taste

2 medium leeks, white and tender green parts, sliced

2 cloves garlic, minced

3 tbsp (42 g) unsalted butter, divided

3 tbsp (24 g) all-purpose flour

2 cups (480 ml) whole milk

¼ tsp freshly grated nutmeg

Preheat the oven to 400°F (200°C).

In a large pot of boiling water, cook the chard in batches until it's wilted, about 1 minute per batch. Drain the chard well and immediately transfer it to a bowl of ice water. Cool slightly. Drain the chard once more, gently squeeze it dry and coarsely chop the leaves and stems together; reserve.

Combine the bread crumbs with 2 tablespoons (30 ml) of olive oil in a medium skillet over medium-high heat and toast, stirring occasionally, until golden and crisp, 10 minutes. Remove from the heat and add the thyme, lemon zest, crushed red pepper and ¼ cup (25 g) of Parmesan. Season to taste with salt and pepper, and reserve in a small bowl. Reserve the skillet.

Wipe out the skillet, and heat the remaining olive oil. Add the leeks, and cook, stirring occasionally, until tender, about 7 minutes. Add the garlic, and cook, stirring, until fragrant, 2 minutes more. Add the reserved chard with a pinch of salt, and remove from the heat. Transfer the greens to a large bowl; reserve the skillet.

Butter a 9-inch (23-cm) pie dish with 1 tablespoon (14 g) of butter. In the reserved skillet, melt the remaining butter over medium heat. Stir in the flour over moderate heat to form a paste. Gradually whisk in the milk, one-third at a time, and cook while whisking until the mixture starts to thicken. Repeat twice more with the remaining milk. Bring the sauce to a boil, whisking constantly. Reduce the heat and simmer, whisking often, until thickened, 10 minutes. Whisk in the remaining Parmesan and the nutmeg. Mix the prepared béchamel sauce into the chard mixture; season with salt and pepper.

Transfer the chard to the prepared pie dish, and top it with the bread crumb mixture. Place the pie dish on a rimmed baking sheet and bake until bubbling, 20 minutes. Allow it to cool slightly before serving.

beans & greens

I have a predilection for humble meals, even more so for those inspired by the garden. Nothing quite fits the bill like a warm and savory pot of homey white beans stewed with dark greens. Feel free to substitute with alternative greens if you have something different on hand.

serves 6

1 lb (454 g) white beans, rinsed and drained

1 quart (1 L) vegetable stock

4 large cloves garlic, peeled and smashed

4 celery stalks, cut into 3" (8-cm) lengths

2 large shallots, halved and peeled

1 sprig of fresh rosemary

1 sprig of fresh thyme

1 bay leaf

1 tsp crushed red pepper

Parmesan rind

1 tbsp (15 ml) extra-virgin olive oil, plus more for serving

1 tsp kosher salt, plus more for seasoning

1 bunch of collard greens, stemmed and coarsely chopped

1 bunch of kale, stemmed and coarsely chopped

Fresh black pepper, to taste

1 tsp fresh lemon juice

Shaved Parmesan, for serving

Put the beans in a large pot and cover them with about 2 inches (5 cm) of cold water. Bring the beans to a boil over high heat. Boil the beans for 1 minute, and then remove them from the heat and cover them. Allow them to sit, covered, for 1 hour.

Drain the beans, and return them to the same pot. Add the vegetable stock and, if necessary, enough water to completely submerge the beans. Add the garlic, celery, shallots, rosemary, thyme, bay leaf, crushed red pepper, Parmesan rind, olive oil and 1 teaspoon of salt. Bring to a boil, reduce the heat and simmer, stirring occasionally, until the beans are tender, about 1 hour. Add additional water, if necessary. Lightly crush some of the beans for a creamy consistency.

Discard the vegetables, herbs and Parmesan rind. Mix in the collard greens and kale, and season with salt and pepper. Cook until the greens have wilted, 5 to 8 minutes. Stir in the lemon juice.

Divide the stew among bowls, and top it with shaved Parmesan and a drizzle of olive oil.

tip: The fall brings a very lush and mature crop of greens such as kale, Swiss chard and collard greens—all staples in my kitchen. Kale is a wise and nutritious choice, as well as an ancestor to vegetables such as cauliflower and broccoli. There are a variety of breeds to choose from, though I often cultivate a curly-leafed variety as well as "cavolo nero," more lovingly dubbed "Dinosaur Kale," a flat, bumpy-leafed variety. It is true that some kale becomes sweeter with the onset of colder temperatures and even snow.

whole eggplant parmesan

The ever-pressing autumn days present a delicious window that bridges between them and the very end of summer. Often, I find this time of year to be the most fruitful. Take advantage of the warm days, cool nights and any eggplants you have producing, and bake them up in the oven with tomato sauce, bread crumbs and plenty of melted mozzarella for a soul-comforting dinner.

serves 6

¾ cup (180 ml) extra-virgin olive oil, divided

4 cloves garlic, thinly sliced

1 (28-oz [794-g]) can whole peeled tomatoes

Pinch of kosher salt, plus more to taste

Pinch of crushed red pepper

4 medium eggplants

Fresh black pepper, to taste

8 sprigs of fresh oregano

8 sprigs of fresh thyme

1½ cups (90 g) coarsely ground fresh bread crumbs

12 oz (340 g) fresh mozzarella, torn into small pieces

1 cup (100 g) Parmesan cheese, finely grated

Preheat the oven to 425°F (218°C).

In a large saucepan over medium-high heat, warm 2 tablespoons (30 ml) of olive oil. Add the sliced garlic, and toast it until it begins to sizzle, 1 to 2 minutes. Add the tomatoes, crushing them with your hands, along with a generous pinch of salt and crushed red pepper. Lower the heat, and simmer the sauce, stirring occasionally, until slightly reduced, about 30 minutes.

Meanwhile, cut each eggplant in half. Score the flesh with the tip of a paring knife in a crosshatch pattern. Transfer the eggplants to two foil-lined rimmed baking sheets, cut side up. Brush each eggplant half with 1 tablespoon (15 ml) of oil, allowing each brushstroke to be fully absorbed before brushing again. Season each half with salt and pepper, and top each with a sprig of oregano and thyme. Transfer to the oven and cook until tender, 35 to 40 minutes. Discard the oregano and thyme.

While the eggplant is roasting, in a medium bowl, toss the bread crumbs with the remaining 2 tablespoons (30 ml) of oil. Transfer the roasted eggplant to two large, shallow baking dishes, cut side up. Top each eggplant half with the prepared tomato sauce, torn mozzarella, the bread crumbs and grated Parmesan. Bake until the bread crumbs are golden and the cheese is bubbling, 25 to 30 minutes. Allow to cool slightly before serving.

autumn slow cooker minestrone with kale, butternut squash & cranberry beans

Overnight soak or quick soak dried cranberry beans for an autumnal take on a minestrone soup. Create the base with a mirepoix of deeply savory leeks, carrots, celery, garlic, thyme and sage, and then throw it into your slow cooker with squash and vegetable stock for an easy, hands-off, cold-night warming soup.

serves 4–6

1 cup (195 g) dried cranberry beans

¼ cup (60 ml) extra-virgin olive oil

2 leeks, halved, white and light green parts, thinly sliced

2 carrots, finely chopped

2 celery stalks, finely chopped

4 cloves garlic, finely chopped

4 sprigs of fresh thyme

4 leaves of fresh sage, minced

1 bay leaf

6 cups (1.4 L) vegetable stock

½ medium butternut squash, peeled, seeded and cut into ½" (1-cm) cubes

1 bunch of kale, stemmed and coarsely chopped

Kosher salt and fresh black pepper, to taste

To soak overnight, place the beans in a large bowl, and add cold water to cover them by 3 inches (8 cm). Cover the bowl, and soak the beans overnight in the refrigerator. If pressed for time, you can do a quick soak by placing the dried beans in a large pot, covering them with water, and bringing them to a boil for 1 minute. Turn the heat off and let the beans soak for 1 hour before draining.

The following day, heat the olive oil in a large skillet over medium-high heat until shimmering. Add the leeks, carrots and celery, and cook until tender, 6 to 8 minutes. Add the garlic, thyme, sage and bay leaf, and cook an additional 2 minutes.

Drain the beans, and add them to your slow cooker. Add the vegetable stock and the cooked vegetable mixture. Add the butternut squash. Cook on low for 6 to 8 hours until the beans and vegetables are very tender. Remove the bay leaf. Before serving, stir in the kale to wilt it. Season to taste with salt and pepper.

butternut squash galette with caramelized onions & blue cheese

Enjoy roasted butternut squash baked into a simple yet rich pastry dough. Deeply golden, slow-cooked onions melt away into a union with sharp and fatty blue cheese, all mixed together with squash. This pastry offers a delightful vegetarian option to end-of-year holidays, dinner parties and get-togethers.

serves 2–4

1 cup (125 g) all-purpose flour, plus more for dusting

1 tsp granulated sugar, divided

¼ tsp kosher salt, plus more to taste

7 tbsp (98 g) cold unsalted butter, cut into ½" (1-cm) pieces, divided

¼ cup (60 ml) ice water

1 small butternut squash (about 1½ lbs [680 g]), peeled, seeded and cut into ½" (1-cm) cubes

2 tbsp (30 ml) extra-virgin olive oil

1 large yellow onion, halved and sliced thin

3 oz (84 g) crumbled blue cheese

Fresh black pepper, to taste

1 egg, lightly beaten

tip: A point to remember is that many squash varieties (including the beloved butternut) are cultivated on vines, which require a large amount of space (rows 16 feet [5 m] apart) in the garden. Hard squash will keep very well in storage, provided you harvest carefully by not ripping or tearing them from the vine.

Preheat the oven to 375°F (190°C).

In a large bowl, combine the flour, ½ teaspoon of sugar and ¼ teaspoon of salt. Using your hands, cut in 3 tablespoons (42 g) of butter until the mixture resembles coarse meal. Cut in another 3 tablespoons (42 g) of butter, and combine until the mixture resembles peas. Drizzle the water over the dough, a little at a time, and knead just until the dough comes together. Pat the dough into a disk, cover it with plastic wrap and refrigerate it for at least 30 minutes and up to 1 hour.

While the dough is chilling, splay the butternut squash out on a large baking sheet. Dot the squash with pieces of the final tablespoon (14 g) of butter, and cover with a sheet of aluminum foil. Roast until tender, about 40 minutes. Allow to cool. Raise the oven's temperature to 400°F (200°C).

While the squash is roasting, heat the olive oil in a large skillet over medium-low heat. Add the onion, remaining ½ teaspoon of sugar and a pinch of salt. Cook, stirring occasionally, until softened and golden, about 20 minutes.

In a large bowl, mix together the roasted squash, caramelized onions and crumbled blue cheese. Season to taste with salt and pepper.

Dust a work surface with flour, and roll out the chilled dough into a 12-inch (30-cm) round. Transfer it to a large parchment-lined baking sheet. Assemble the squash mixture over the middle of the dough, leaving a 1-inch (3-cm) border. Fold the border over the filling, pleating the edges and leaving the center open.

Beat the egg with 1 tablespoon (15 ml) of water, and brush the pastry with the egg wash. Bake until golden brown, 30 to 40 minutes. Allow to cool before slicing and serving.

swiss chard tacos with chili-lime pepitas & queso fresco

Sautéed Swiss chard with chipotle and fresh corn wilts smoothly into a silky-savory filling for tacos. Top your tortillas with plenty of lime, chili-spiked pumpkin seeds and a brush of creamy queso fresco for a delicious vegetarian meal.

serves 4–6

½ cup (70 g) raw pepitas

1 tbsp (15 ml) fresh lime juice

½ tsp chili powder

Pinch of kosher salt, plus more to taste

2 tbsp (30 ml) extra-virgin olive oil

1 bunch of Swiss chard, stems finely diced and leaves sliced into ribbons, separated

1 white onion, thinly sliced

2 cloves garlic, minced

2 chipotle peppers in adobo sauce, finely chopped, plus 1 tsp adobo sauce

2 ears of corn, kernels removed (about 1 cup [144 g])

Fresh black pepper, to taste

8 warm corn tortillas

½ cup (61 g) crumbled queso fresco, for serving

Fresh cilantro, for serving

Lime, for serving

Stir together the pepitas, lime juice, chili powder and a pinch of salt. Heat the pepitas in a large skillet over medium heat, stirring occasionally, until toasted, about 4 minutes; reserve.

Heat the olive oil in a large skillet with a lid over medium-high heat. Add the Swiss chard stems, onion and garlic, and cook, stirring occasionally, until tender, 6 to 8 minutes. Stir in the chipotle peppers, adobo sauce, corn and Swiss chard leaves. Cover the skillet, and cook, stirring occasionally, until the chard has wilted and the corn is tender, 5 minutes. Season to taste with salt and pepper.

Serve warm corn tortillas topped with the Swiss chard mixture, chili pepitas, queso fresco, cilantro and lime.

tip: Swiss chard, a relative of beets and another favorite, is a force to be reckoned with come autumn. Bright Lights is a coveted variety that produces electric neon stalks and deep, glossy leaves that are eager to please. Chard is one of the few greens tolerant of both the heat and cold, buying it a decent amount of time to mature. Feel free to sow chard in the spring to enjoy it all season long. Harvest it weekly once the leaves are anywhere from 6 to 8 inches (15 to 20 cm) long and from the outside in, allowing the heart of the plant to continue producing.

butternut squash ice cream with coconut & lemongrass

The natural sweetness of butternut squash, tempted out even more by roasting it, makes it an exceptional candidate for homemade ice cream. With creamy, fatty coconut milk, deeply toasted coconut shreds and aromatic lemongrass, this makes for a delicious and indulgent treat, perfect for the days of fall.

makes 1 quart (1 L)

1 small butternut squash (about 1½ lbs [680 g]), peeled, seeded and cut into 2" (5-cm) pieces

1 tbsp (14 g) unsalted butter

½ cup (38 g) shredded unsweetened coconut

4 stalks lemongrass

1 cup (240 ml) unsweetened coconut milk

1 cup (240 ml) whole milk

1 cup (240 ml) heavy cream

¾ cup (144 g) granulated sugar

¼ tsp kosher salt

5 egg yolks

Preheat the oven to 350°F (175°C).

Splay the butternut squash out on a large roasting pan, dot with pieces of the butter and cover with a sheet of aluminum foil. Roast until tender, about 40 minutes. Allow the squash to cool for 15 minutes. Purée until smooth, and add to a large bowl; reserve 1½ cups (360 ml).

In a medium saucepan, toast the shredded coconut over medium heat until golden, about 4 minutes. Transfer the coconut to a plate; reserve the saucepan.

Prepare the lemongrass by smashing it with a rolling pin to release the flavor. Slice the stalks into 1-inch (3-cm) pieces.

In the reserved saucepan, combine the toasted coconut, lemongrass, coconut milk, whole milk, heavy cream, sugar and salt. Bring to a simmer, and remove from the heat once the sugar completely dissolves, about 5 minutes.

In a medium bowl, whisk together the egg yolks until smooth. Whisking constantly, slowly pour the warm cream mixture into the egg yolks. Return everything back to the pot, and cook over medium-low heat until the mixture is thick enough to coat the back of a spoon, about 170°F (75°C). Do not allow it to boil.

Allow the custard to steep for 1 hour. Strain it through a fine-mesh sieve into the bowl with the squash purée. Discard the solids. Whisk to combine everything until smooth. Cover and chill at least 4 hours or overnight.

Process in an ice cream machine according to the manufacturer's instructions. Serve directly from the machine for a soft-serve consistency, or place the ice cream in the freezer to further freeze it.

winter

Much of this season I spend tending to the garden to ensure a productive future. If you choose to rest your beds, take the time to remove old stalks and vines. Consider growing a cover crop in the fall before the first frost, such as clover, which enriches your soil and attracts beneficial insects. Simply turn it into the dirt the following spring. Always pay attention to your soil: it is the genesis of a healthy and productive season. Replenish lost nutrients with compost and earthworms.

Seeds and seed catalogs nurse my waning smile on the bleakest winter days. Although it's quiet in the garden, these moments are perfect for planning ahead. Consider journaling throughout the year so you may study your garden's successes and failures.

An excellent practice is saving seeds. Perhaps you'd like to repeat certain triumphs. If you take the time to save the seeds from your harvest, you will be rewarded with future plants suited to your growing conditions. Start always with seeds from open-pollinated plants. Collect mature seedpods, often already dried, and gently crush and shake them out to collect the seeds. Wet-fruited crops, such as tomatoes and squash, will need to be kept on the vine until a bit overripe, so choose one handsome specimen for the job. Remove the seeds, scraping away as much flesh as possible, and add them to a jar of water. Once the seeds sink you can drain them and scatter them on newspaper to dry. Save your seeds in a cool, dark, dry area.

As we move indoors, we look toward the fare that will keep us warm until the spring arrives again. My favorites include the Roasted Beet Dip with Walnuts, Dill and Horseradish (page 140); the Double Celery Soup with Salted Yogurt and Pesto (page 160), especially when using Celery Leaf Pesto (page 147); and a strong case for parsnips, the Parsnip Cake with Rosemary-Maple-Tahini Glaze (page 167).

roasted cauliflower with olives & capers

Once winter settles in, I turn to my oven for roasted vegetables multiple times a week. A favorite preparation is deeply browning cauliflower and then giving it a final but hearty toss with buttery walnuts, briny olives and capers, fresh parsley and bright lemon zest. Serve this as a companion to a larger main, or enjoy it all on its own. Try pairing this meal with a frittata; a large, leafy salad; or perhaps as a side with the Seared Cauliflower and Potato Soup with Capers and Bread Crumbs (page 156) for an added dose of cauliflower.

serves 4

1 lb (454 g) cauliflower, trimmed and cut into bite-size florets

2 tbsp (30 ml) extra-virgin olive oil

Pinch of kosher salt

Pinch of crushed red pepper

¼ cup (30 g) walnut halves

⅓ cup (60 g) kalamata olives, pitted

2 tbsp (6 g) fresh flat-leaf parsley

1 tbsp (9 g) capers, drained and rinsed

½ tsp finely grated lemon zest

Preheat the oven to 425°F (218°C).

On a large rimmed baking sheet, toss the cauliflower with the olive oil, a pinch of salt and a pinch of crushed red pepper. Roast until the cauliflower begins to brown, 20 minutes. Add the walnuts, olives, parsley, capers and lemon zest, and toss before roasting for an additional 10 minutes.

roasted beet dip with walnuts, dill & horseradish

Earthy, roasted beets (and beets in general) are one of life's greatest pleasures. Whir them up and transform them into a dip with some of their greatest complementary flavors—walnuts, dill and horseradish. Serve this dip cool with pita, crackers or additional raw, sliced vegetables.

serves 4–6

1 lb (454 g) medium red beets, scrubbed and trimmed

2 tbsp (30 ml) extra-virgin olive oil, plus more for processing

½ cup (60 g) walnut halves

2 cloves garlic

¼ cup (61 g) plain Greek yogurt

2 tbsp (30 ml) lemon juice

2 tbsp (6 g) chopped fresh dill, plus more for serving

2 tbsp (6 g) chopped fresh flat-leaf parsley

2 tsp (10 g) prepared horseradish

Kosher salt, to taste

Preheat the oven to 350°F (175°C).

Place the beets in a baking dish, and drizzle them with 2 tablespoons (30 ml) of olive oil. Add ¼ cup (60 ml) of water to the bottom of the baking dish, and cover it with foil. Bake the beets until they are knife-tender, about 1 hour.

During the last 10 minutes of roasting, place the walnut halves on a small sheet pan in a single layer. Roast until they begin to turn golden and smell fragrant. Cool.

Cool the roasted beets slightly. Once cool enough to handle, peel the skins and quarter them. Add the beets to a food processor along with the toasted walnuts, garlic, Greek yogurt, lemon juice, dill, parsley and horseradish. Stream in olive oil while processing until the dip is smooth; season with salt.

tip: Ever notice how beet seeds have a somewhat crinkled appearance? This is because they are considered a multigerm seed. Seeds like this germinate multiple seedlings at once, making it imperative to thin beets down after sowing them. Thin young, 1-inch (3-cm) seedlings to 3 to 4 inches (8 to 10 cm) apart. Harvest baby beets at about 1 inch (3 cm) across, or full-size beets at about 4 to 5 inches (10 to 13 cm) across.

burnt parsnips with harissa-spiced maple syrup

Parsnips present themselves as an often underappreciated root vegetable. Rejuvenate their reputation with an irresistibly sticky, sweet and spicy glaze. Maple syrup and harissa paste fuse together and caramelize on the parsnips for a delicious treat. Serve these parsnips as a side dish or as a roasted component to a bed of cooked grains. Try pairing them as a side to the Swiss Chard Gratin (page 123) for some vegetarian holiday ideas.

serves 4

1½ lbs (680 g) parsnips, peeled and cut into 4" (10-cm) pieces

1 tbsp (15 ml) extra-virgin olive oil

Kosher salt and fresh black pepper, to taste

1 clove garlic, minced

2 tbsp (28 g) unsalted butter, melted and slightly cooled

2 tbsp (30 ml) pure maple syrup

1 tbsp (16 g) harissa paste

Preheat the oven to 425°F (218°C).

On a large foil-lined baking sheet, toss the parsnips with the olive oil; season with salt and pepper. Roast, tossing occasionally, until tender and charred in spots, 20 to 25 minutes.

Meanwhile, in a small bowl, whisk together the garlic, butter, maple syrup and harissa paste.

Remove the parsnips from the oven, add the garlic mixture and toss to coat. Roast, tossing occasionally, until the parsnips are completely tender and caramelized, 8 to 10 minutes.

tip: Parsnips are sweetest and best harvested following a few hard frosts. However, in fairly mild zones you can leave parsnips to grow in the ground all winter, provided you mulch and cover their tops. If you do, harvest them first thing the following spring.

fried sunchoke chips with lemon-thyme salt

Sunchokes, also known as Jerusalem artichokes, are an interesting tuber to cultivate, reaching a marked sweetness come winter. An actual relative of the sunflower, they take well to many preparations, including raw and sliced, roasted and mashed. Here I treat it like a fried chip made addictive with fresh thyme- and lemon-infused salt.

serves 6

2 lbs (907 g) sunchokes, scrubbed and patted dry

Vegetable oil, for frying

1 tbsp (8 g) kosher salt

2 tsp (2 g) minced fresh thyme

½ tsp freshly grated lemon zest

Carefully slice the sunchokes into thin rounds.

Pour enough oil into a medium pot for it to come halfway up the side. Heat the oil to 375°F (190°C). While heating, mix together the salt, thyme and lemon zest. Rub them together with your fingers until fragrant and blended.

Working in batches, fry the sunchoke slices until golden brown, turning them over occasionally, 3 to 5 minutes. Transfer them to a paper towel–lined plate and immediately season with the infused salt.

celery leaf pesto

Be sure to reserve your celery leaves! They are responsible for great flavor that is only accentuated by an indulgent combination of olive oil, pistachios, Parmesan, garlic and lemon. Make this savory pesto to have on hand and use as you would any other. Dollop this on top of the Double Celery Soup with Salted Yogurt and Pesto (page 160) for a delicious match.

serves 4

1 cup (40 g) packed flat-leaf parsley leaves

1 cup (40 g) packed celery leaves

1 cup (120 g) dry-roasted pistachios

¾ cup (180 ml) extra-virgin olive oil

¼ cup (25 g) finely grated Parmesan cheese

3 cloves garlic

1 tsp lemon zest

Kosher salt and black pepper, to taste

Process the parsley, celery leaves, pistachios, olive oil, Parmesan cheese, garlic and lemon zest in a food processor until smooth. Season to taste with salt and pepper.

all-purpose vegetable stock

A good stock is essential for crafting giant pots of soup, a nourishing practice I repeat weekly in the colder months. Find here my go-to vegetable stock, crafted from often neglected refrigerator denizens whose only destiny is soup broth. A savory and sweet combination of celery, carrots, fennel, leek, onion, garlic and herbs is tied together with rich and meaty mushrooms for a flavorful, all-purpose elixir. Feel free to use this stock for any of the soup recipes in this book.

makes 7 cups (1.7 L)

½ cup (38 g) button mushrooms, halved if large

3 stalks celery, roughly chopped

2 carrots, roughly chopped

1 fennel bulb, roughly chopped

1 leek, halved

1 large yellow onion, left unpeeled and quartered

1 head garlic, halved crosswise

6 sprigs of fresh parsley

6 sprigs of fresh thyme

2 bay leaves

1 tbsp (8 g) whole black peppercorns

1 tsp kosher salt

1 tsp fennel seeds

1 tsp coriander seeds

Combine the mushrooms, celery, carrots, fennel, leek, onion, garlic, parsley, thyme, bay leaves, peppercorns, salt, fennel seeds and coriander seeds in a pot and cover with 2 quarts (2 L) of water. Bring to a boil over medium-high heat, then reduce to a simmer for 1 hour. Strain the stock through a fine-mesh sieve into a large bowl, pressing the vegetables against the side of the strainer to release their juices, and discard the solids.

Allow the stock to cool at room temperature for 1 hour. Cover the stock, and transfer it to the refrigerator to chill completely. The stock will keep for about 1 week refrigerated. Alternatively, freeze it to always have it on hand.

tip: Autumn and winter signify onion and garlic planting season. If you've never cultivated garlic, I urge you to try it, as it remains one of the easiest crops. Try getting your garlic head from a nursery instead of the grocery store. Plant unpeeled, large cloves of garlic with the root end down 2 to 4 inches (5 to 10 cm) deep, depending on how hard your winter is. It is often wise to lightly mulch the top of the bed. The greatest feeling is discovering their first green shoots with the arrival of spring, a deeply welcome sign.

roasted red onions with balsamic & rosemary

As humble as it may be, the onion is a companion to almost everything I cook—in this I am surely not alone. Here I let them stand on their own, roasted whole until delightfully caramelized beneath a blanket of butter, sweetly thickened balsamic and savory rosemary, which elevates their flavor effortlessly. Serve these roasted onions as a side dish, perhaps paired nicely with a risotto.

serves 6

6 tbsp (84 g) unsalted butter

¼ cup (60 ml) balsamic vinegar

4 large red onions, halved

4 sprigs of fresh rosemary

Kosher salt and fresh black pepper, to taste

Preheat the oven to 350°F (175°C).

In a small saucepot over medium heat, combine the butter and vinegar. Bring to a gentle boil and cook, stirring occasionally, until the mixture reduces slightly, 2 minutes.

Place the onions in a baking dish, cut side up, in a single layer and snugly against one another. Divide the sprigs of rosemary across the onion halves. Drizzle the butter mixture over the top, and roast until softened and caramelized, 35 to 40 minutes. Season to taste with salt and pepper.

tip: Select your onion varieties depending on your geography and how much daylight you get. Onions are often classified as long-day, intermediate-day or short-day. A good bet for most gardeners are intermediate-day onions, which begin to bulb when the daylight peaks at 12- to 14-hour days.

curry-honey roasted winter vegetables

Roast up a golden mix of some of winter's finest vegetables slathered in a sticky, sweet and spicy curry-honey glaze. Feel free to adapt this mix to whatever abundance you may have on hand. Serve it as a delicious cold-weather side, or make a larger meal out of it by pairing it with salad greens and your favorite cooked grain.

serves 6–8

¼ cup (60 ml) extra-virgin olive oil

¼ cup (60 ml) honey

1 tsp curry powder

2 large carrots, sliced ½" (1 cm) thick

1 large parsnip, sliced ½" (1 cm) thick

1 large sweet potato, peeled and cut into ½" (1-cm) cubes

1 medium butternut squash (about 1½ lbs [680 g]), peeled, seeded and cut into ½" (1-cm) cubes

1 lb (454 g) golden beets, peeled and sliced ½" (1 cm) thick

2 medium red onions, quartered

2 tsp (2 g) chopped fresh thyme

Kosher salt and fresh black pepper, to taste

Fresh lemon juice, for serving

Preheat the oven to 425°F (218°C).

In a large bowl, whisk together the olive oil, honey and curry powder. Add the carrots, parsnip, sweet potato, squash, beets, red onions and thyme, and toss to coat; season with salt and pepper. Divide the vegetables between two large baking sheets. Cover both sheets with aluminum foil. Roast, switching shelves and stirring halfway through, until the vegetables are tender and caramelized, 40 minutes. Remove the foil, and continue to roast an additional 10 minutes until the vegetables are glazed. Serve warm with a squeeze of lemon juice.

celery root and apple slaw

Winter can occasionally have the tendency to appeal to one too many heavy and hot roasted dishes. Savor a lighter winter approach with a raw slaw composed of celery root, celery, apple and scallions. Peppered with herbs and sunflower seeds, and dressed with tangy mustard, vinegar and horseradish, this slaw can be used to complement or brighten weightier meals. Try serving it alongside the Double Celery Soup with Salted Yogurt and Pesto (page 160), or as a condiment to your favorite veggie burger.

serves 4

¼ cup (60 ml) extra-virgin olive oil

2 tbsp (32 g) Dijon mustard

2 tbsp (30 ml) apple cider vinegar

2 tsp (10 g) prepared horseradish

1 tsp honey

½ tsp caraway seeds

Kosher salt and fresh black pepper, to taste

½ lb (227 g) celery root, peeled and julienned

1 large green apple, cored and julienned

3 celery ribs, thinly sliced, celery leaves reserved

1 bunch of scallions, sliced thin on the bias

½ cup (20 g) fresh flat-leaf parsley, finely chopped

2 tbsp (6 g) fresh oregano, finely chopped

½ cup (70 g) sunflower seeds

In a large bowl, whisk together the olive oil, Dijon mustard, apple cider vinegar, horseradish, honey and caraway seeds. Season with salt and pepper. Add the celery root, apple, celery ribs, reserved celery leaves, scallions, parsley, oregano and sunflower seeds. Toss to combine.

seared cauliflower & potato soup with capers & bread crumbs

The combination of cauliflower and potatoes is responsible for an admirably smooth soup, a comforting meal on a cold and snowy day. Searing the cauliflower beforehand lends a sweet and slightly smoky note, which translates well into the final soup. Finish each bowl with a sprinkling of savory, golden bread crumbs studded with lemon, red pepper, Parmesan and capers.

serves 4–6

½ cup (120 ml) extra-virgin olive oil, divided, plus more for serving

1 large head cauliflower (2 lb [907 g]), cut into 2" (5-cm) florets

1 tsp kosher salt, divided, plus more to taste

3 tbsp (42 g) unsalted butter

1 large yellow onion, diced

1 small fennel bulb, chopped

6 cloves garlic, minced, divided

¼ tsp crushed red pepper

½ lb (227 g) potatoes, diced small

1 quart (1 L) low-sodium vegetable stock

¼ tsp finely grated lemon zest

1½ tbsp (22 ml) fresh lemon juice

Fresh black pepper, to taste

2 tbsp (18 g) capers, rinsed and patted dry

¾ cup (45 g) fresh coarse bread crumbs

¼ cup (10 g) fresh chopped flat-leaf parsley

Grated Parmesan, for serving

Heat 2 tablespoons (30 ml) of olive oil in a large pot over medium-high heat. Add half of the cauliflower to cover the bottom of the pot in a single layer, making sure not to overcrowd. Cook, undisturbed, for 3 to 4 minutes, or until browned on one side. Transfer to a bowl, and repeat with another 2 tablespoons (30 ml) of oil and the remaining cauliflower. Season all of the seared cauliflower with ½ teaspoon of salt.

In the same pot, melt the butter and add the onion, fennel, half of the minced garlic, the crushed red pepper and ½ teaspoon of salt. Cook until the onion has softened and starts to become translucent. Add the potatoes and vegetable stock. Bring to a simmer, cover the pot and cook until the potatoes are just tender, 15 minutes. Add the cauliflower, cover once more and cook until tender, 10 minutes. Add the lemon zest, and purée the soup in a blender. Return the soup to the pot, and stir in the lemon juice; season to taste with salt and pepper.

Meanwhile, heat the remaining ¼ cup (60 ml) of olive oil in a small saucepan over medium-low heat. Add the remaining garlic, and cook, stirring occasionally, until just golden, 3 to 5 minutes. Add the capers, and cook until they begin to pop, 2 to 3 minutes. Add the bread crumbs and parsley, and toss to coat. Cook, stirring often, until the bread crumbs are golden, 2 to 3 minutes.

Serve the soup topped with the bread crumb mixture, grated Parmesan and a drizzle of olive oil.

turnip soup with leeks, potato & cheddar-scallion frico

This soup pays respect to one of winter's most unassuming, meek contenders—the turnip. In a trinity with the leek and potato, it evokes a classic but humble flavor, perfectly suited for cold days. Top each bowl with lacy cheddar crackers for a gratifying and delicious bite.

serves 6–8

2 tbsp (28 g) unsalted butter

3 medium leeks, white and pale green parts, sliced

Pinch of kosher salt, plus more to taste

1½ lb (680 g) turnips, peeled and diced

1 large russet potato (¾ lb [340 g]), peeled and diced

6 cups (1.4 L) low-sodium vegetable stock

1 bay leaf

4 sprigs of fresh thyme

1 cup (120 g) finely grated aged cheddar cheese

3 scallions, finely minced

Fresh black pepper, to taste

Melt the butter in a large soup pot over medium-high heat, and add the leeks with a small pinch of salt. Cook, stirring, until tender, 5 to 7 minutes. Add the turnips, potato, vegetable stock, bay leaf and thyme; season with salt. Bring to a boil, reduce the heat, cover and simmer for 45 minutes, or until the vegetables are very tender. Remove from the heat, and discard the bay leaf and thyme sprigs.

Meanwhile, preheat the oven to 375°F (190°C). In a medium bowl, mix together the cheddar and scallions. Cover two large baking sheets with antislip pads or parchment paper. Spoon about 2 tablespoons (7 g) of the cheddar mixture onto each baking sheet, and spread it into a 4-inch (10-cm) round. Repeat with the remaining cheese, leaving about 2 inches (5 cm) in between each round. One sheet at a time, bake until the cheese is melted and its edges are beginning to brown, 6 to 8 minutes. Carefully remove the cheese with a spatula, immediately drape it over a rolling pin or clean bottle, and let it cool in a curved shape before transferring it to a plate. Repeat with the remaining cheese.

Purée the soup, in batches if necessary, in a blender until completely smooth. Return it to the soup pot to warm. Adjust the salt and pepper if necessary. Serve the soup warm and garnished with a cheddar-scallion frico.

double celery soup with salted yogurt & pesto

Winter dares to invite the humblest of vegetables, offering a unique challenge to include them in cooking. Here the celery root is a deeply savored guest. Cooking the knobby root down with leeks, herbs and celery stalks creates a silky soup sure to warm the coldest bones. Pair it with a dollop of Celery Leaf Pesto (page 147) for a genuinely great, triple-celery soup.

serves 6

2 tbsp (28 g) unsalted butter

1 tbsp (15 ml) extra-virgin olive oil

2 large leeks, halved, white and pale green parts, thinly sliced

1 medium celery root (about 1 lb [454 g]), peeled and diced

6 celery ribs, halved and sliced

3 sprigs of fresh thyme

2 bay leaves

6 cups (1.4 L) vegetable stock

1 cup (245 g) whole-milk Greek yogurt, at room temperature

Pinch of kosher salt

Fresh black pepper, for serving

¼ cup (60 ml) Celery Leaf Pesto (page 147), for serving

Buttered toast, for serving

Melt the butter and olive oil in a large, heavy-bottomed pot over medium-high heat. Add the leeks, and sauté until just tender, 6 to 8 minutes. Stir in the celery root, celery ribs and thyme. Add the bay leaves and stock, and bring to a boil. Reduce the heat, cover and gently simmer until all of the vegetables are tender, 25 minutes. Discard the thyme and bay leaves. Working in batches, purée the soup until smooth in a blender. Return the soup to the pot to keep it warm.

Meanwhile, in a medium bowl, stir together the yogurt and a generous pinch of salt.

Serve the soup hot with a dollop of yogurt, freshly ground black pepper, a topping of Celery Leaf Pesto and planks of buttered toast for a comforting winter meal.

baked whole-wheat orzo with brussels sprouts & fontina

The cold months undoubtedly spur a natural gravitation toward comfort-food dishes, such as this creamy baked orzo with Brussels sprouts and cheese. Perhaps made slightly virtuous with whole-wheat orzo and pan-roasted Brussels sprouts, the pine nuts, mozzarella and Fontina richly round it back out. No need to precook the orzo: it will hydrate in the oven and get satisfyingly crisp on top.

serves 4–6

1 lb (454 g) Brussels sprouts

1 tbsp (14 g) unsalted butter

2 tbsp (30 ml) extra-virgin olive oil, divided

4 large cloves garlic, slivered

¼ cup (30 g) pine nuts

Pinch of kosher salt

1 large onion, coarsely chopped

½ lb (227 g) orzo

1½ cups (360 ml) vegetable stock

4 oz (113 g) shredded Fontina cheese

2 oz (57 g) fresh mozzarella cheese, diced

2 tbsp (6 g) minced fresh thyme

1 tsp freshly grated lemon zest

Fresh black pepper, to taste

½ cup (30 g) bread crumbs

¼ cup (25 g) grated Parmesan cheese

Preheat the oven to 375°F (190°C).

Trim the Brussels sprouts and halve them lengthwise; divide the largest sprouts into quarters. Melt the butter with 1 tablespoon (15 ml) of olive oil in a large skillet over medium-high heat. Add the garlic, and cook, stirring constantly, until pale golden; remove to a large bowl. Reduce the heat to medium-low, and add the Brussels sprouts to the skillet, cut sides down, in a single layer. Add the pine nuts and a pinch of salt. Cook the sprouts, undisturbed, until the undersides are golden and crisp-tender, 12 to 15 minutes. Add the Brussels sprouts to the bowl with the garlic, and wipe out the skillet.

Heat the remaining tablespoon (15 ml) of olive oil in the skillet over medium-high heat. Add the onion, and sauté until tender, 5 minutes. Stir in the orzo, and toast an additional minute.

Add the onion and orzo to the bowl with the Brussels sprouts and garlic. Add the vegetable stock, Fontina, mozzarella, thyme and lemon zest, and mix well to combine. Season with black pepper.

Transfer the mixture to a 2-quart (2-L) baking dish. Cover with aluminum foil, and bake for 20 minutes. While the orzo is baking, combine the bread crumbs with the Parmesan cheese. Remove the foil, sprinkle the bread crumbs over the top of the pasta and bake an additional 20 minutes uncovered. Allow to rest for 5 to 10 minutes before serving.

parmesan-baked parsnip gnocchi with marinara

This baked dish boasts a unique method for preparing parsnips—offering a welcomed departure from their usual roast. Bake a few alongside a potato and gently fold the two together to form an easy gnocchi dough.

serves 4–6

¾ lb (340 g) russet potatoes

¾ lb (340 g) parsnips

¼ cup (60 ml) plus 1 tsp extra-virgin olive oil, divided

1 (28-oz [794-g]) can whole San Marzano tomatoes

6 cloves garlic, peeled and slivered

Pinch of crushed red pepper

1 tsp kosher salt, plus more to taste

2 sprigs of fresh basil

1 large egg yolk, beaten

1½–2 cups (188–250 g) all-purpose flour, plus more for dusting

½ cup (56 g) shredded mozzarella

½ cup (40 g) shredded Parmesan

Preheat the oven to 400°F (200°C). Prick the potatoes gently a few times with a fork. Place the whole potatoes and parsnips on a wire rack atop a large baking sheet, and coat them with a teaspoon of olive oil. Roast until fork-tender, about 1 hour. Allow to cool enough to handle. Reduce the oven temperature to 375°F (190°C).

While the vegetables are roasting, make the marinara. Add the tomatoes and their juices to a large bowl, and crush them with your hands. Add 1 cup (240 ml) of water to the empty tomato can, and gently rinse the sides to get the remaining tomato juices; reserve.

Heat the remaining ¼ cup (60 ml) of olive oil in a large skillet over medium heat until shimmering. Add the garlic, and cook until sizzling but before it begins to brown. Add the crushed tomatoes and the can of water. Add a pinch of crushed red pepper and 1 teaspoon of salt. Add the sprigs of basil to the surface of the sauce, simmer for a minute until they wilt, and then submerge them into the sauce. Simmer the sauce until thickened, 15 minutes; reserve.

Pass the potatoes through a ricer or a food mill fitted with the finest disc, discarding the skins. Add the parsnips to a food processor, and purée until smooth. Turn the potatoes and parsnips out onto a work surface together, season with salt and continue to cool.

Add the egg yolk to the potato-parsnip mixture, and sprinkle in ¾ cup (94 g) flour. Gather the mixture together, gently kneading and adding additional flour, just until the dough comes together. Overworking or overflouring the dough will result in a heavy gnocchi. Divide the dough into three equal pieces and lightly flour your work surface and hands. Roll each piece into a rope ½ inch (1 cm) thick, and cut each rope into pieces ½ inch (1 cm) long.

Bring a large pot of salted water to a boil. Boil the gnocchi in batches. The gnocchi will initially sink and then rise back to the top; cook for an additional minute and drain. Add the boiled and drained gnocchi to a medium baking dish. Cover with some of the prepared marinara sauce, and sprinkle with the mozzarella and Parmesan. Transfer the baking dish to the oven, and bake until warmed and the cheese has melted, 6 to 8 minutes. Finish beneath the broiler for a crisp, golden top.

parsnip cake with rosemary-maple-tahini glaze

If you're faced with a glut of parsnips, may I wholeheartedly suggest you bake them into this cake—which could possibly be my favorite recipe in this book. They work well to ensure the cake is moist and adhere smoothly to a cast of warming winter flavors such as cinnamon, maple syrup, tahini and rosemary. I encourage you to bake this sweet and spicy cake often and enjoy it any time of the day.

makes 1 (9 × 5" [23 × 13-cm]) loaf with extra maple syrup

cake
1½ cups (188 g) all-purpose flour
1¾ tsp (7 g) baking powder
1 tsp kosher salt
½ tsp cinnamon
¼ tsp baking soda
½ cup (123 g) plain Greek yogurt
½ cup (140 g) tahini
3 large eggs, at room temperature
1 cup (192 g) granulated sugar
2 tsp (10 ml) vanilla extract
¼ cup (60 ml) olive oil
1 cup (130 g) coarsely grated parsnip
½ cup (60 g) walnuts, coarsely chopped

rosemary maple syrup
½ cup (120 ml) maple syrup
2 sprigs of fresh rosemary

glaze
½ cup (65 g) confectioners' sugar
2 tbsp (30 ml) Rosemary Maple Syrup
2 tbsp (35 g) tahini
2 tbsp (30 ml) water

Preheat the oven to 350°F (175°C). Lightly oil and flour a 9 × 5" (23 × 13–cm) loaf pan.

In a small bowl, whisk together the flour, baking powder, kosher salt, cinnamon and baking soda. In a separate small bowl, whisk together the yogurt and tahini until smooth.

Using an electric mixer on medium-high speed, beat the eggs, granulated sugar and vanilla extract together in a large bowl until the mixture is light and fluffy, about 4 minutes. With the mixer running, gradually drizzle in the olive oil, and then add the yogurt-tahini mixture. Fold in the flour mixture with a rubber spatula until just combined. Fold in the parsnip and the walnuts.

Pour the batter into the prepared pan, and spread it into an even layer. Bake until a cake tester or toothpick inserted in the center comes out clean, 60 to 65 minutes. Let the cake cool slightly in the pan, and then turn it out onto a wire rack to cool completely.

Meanwhile, in a small saucepan, combine the maple syrup and the rosemary. Bring to a boil, reduce to a simmer, cover and cook over medium-low heat for 6 to 8 minutes. Remove from the heat. Allow the mixture to steep an additional 10 minutes, and then discard the rosemary.

To make the glaze, whisk the confectioners' sugar, Rosemary Maple Syrup, tahini and water together in a medium bowl. Drizzle onto the cooled cake.

thank you

Writing a book is a labor of love and a child of passion, such that would cease to flourish without the expertise, confidence, encouragement and hearts of many.

Words cannot express my gratitude for the readers and friends I've made along the way. Thank you for your unending support, even on the coldest of winter days.

Thank you deeply to my family and my mother and father for your unwavering dedication and enthusiasm.

All of my love to Victoria for being a voice of reason and fielding all of my frantic wonderments, even from China.

Thank you Jason for your patience and support—you helped me breathe when I was convinced there was no oxygen.

Lastly, this book would not have been possible without the steadfast devotion of the team at Page Street Publishing. Thank you, Will and Lauren, for believing in me. Thank you, Lauren, for your genuine voice and caring commitment. Thank you Meg, Laura and the design team, for visualizing something so beautiful.

a portrait of the artist as a young woman

Danielle Majeika is a Virginian turned Californian turned Midwesterner dreaming of Appalachia again. When she isn't gripping the earth she's thinking about humble and inventive ways to cook it and poetic ways to contemplate it.

Visit her at www.theperpetualseason.com

index